T0064615

"Grandma, I Lost the Pass Code to My Brain!"

Nine Keys to Better Tomorrows for You
and Your Children

LOIS DAPPEN HINKLY

BALBOA.
PRESS

A DIVISION OF HAY HOUSE

Balboa Press books may be ordered through booksellers or by contacting:

Balboa Press
A Division of Hay House
1663 Liberty Drive
Bloomington, IN 47403
www.balboapress.com
1 (877) 407-4847

Because of the dynamic nature of the Internet, any web addresses or links contained in this book may have changed since publication and may no longer be valid. The views expressed in this work are solely those of the author and do not necessarily reflect the views of the publisher, and the publisher hereby disclaims any responsibility for them.

The author of this book does not dispense medical advice or prescribe the use of any technique as a form of treatment for physical, emotional, or medical problems without the advice of a physician, either directly or indirectly. The intent of the author is only to offer information of a general nature to help you in your quest for emotional and spiritual well-being. In the event you use any of the information in this book for yourself, which is your constitutional right, the author and the publisher assume no responsibility for your actions.

Any people depicted in stock imagery provided by Thinkstock are models, and such images are being used for illustrative purposes only.
Certain stock imagery © Thinkstock.

Print information available on the last page.

ISBN: 978-1-5043-3377-1 (sc)
ISBN: 978-1-5043-3378-8 (e)

Balboa Press rev. date: 06/29/2015

Contents

Acknowledgments...vii

Introduction...ix

Chapter 1 The First Key for Better Tomorrows:
Learn to Listen with Your Heart.....................................1
How to Raise Your "Listening from the
Heart" Intelligence... 10

Chapter 2 The Second Key for Better Tomorrows:
Expand Your Perspective 15
How to Build Self Confidence....................................27

Chapter 3 The Third Key for Better Tomorrows:
Know That You Matter 30
Lessons on how to Validate Your Self and Your Child ... 39

Chapter 4 The Fourth Key for Better Tomorrows:
Trust What Lies Within You 45
Start to Determine your Self Preference Classifications.. 56

Chapter 5 The Fifth Key for Better Tomorrows:
Raise Your Natural You Awareness 58
Your Own Talent Bank (Based on Your First
Identity—Your Birth Date) 64

Chapter 6 The Sixth Key for Better Tomorrows:
          Be Open to the Coincidences of Your Name Legacy..... 75
          The Magic of Your Given Name Characteristics 79

Chapter 7 The Seventh Key for Better Tomorrows:
          Remember to Turn! Turn! Turn!.................................... 94
          The "Nine-Year Cycle" Theory of Growth
              and Change... 98

Chapter 8 The Eighth Key for Better Tomorrows:
          Educate Yourself Before Choosing Your Next Steps!....114
          How to Raise Your Thought and Action Energy..........119

Chapter 9 The Ninth Key for Better Tomorrows:
          Commit to Loving the Child within You So
          You Can Inspire the Child in front of You 130
          Simple Positive Actions to Enrich Character................ 140

Acknowledgments

I am very grateful for the people in my life who have taught me how to be.

I would not be who I am without the influence of my parents, Ted and Dorothy Wuster Dappen. Not only was I lucky enough to have parents who held children and education in high esteem, but my older siblings and their spouses also encouraged me to follow in their "teacher" footsteps. All four of my brothers (Joe, Bob, Gene, and Leon) and three of their wives (Betty, Barb, Judy and my first husband's sister-- Trixie Vant) were teachers. My sister, Ardie, was a master of unconditionally loving all people. She was a wonderful model for me to see all children as lovable and capable.

My daughter, Erika, is my greatest teacher and promoter through thick and thin. All 11 of my grandchildren—including the one who lost her pass code—have been exceptional teachers and my inspiration for wanting better tomorrows for all children.

My husband, Ray, was a teacher and a principal before his stroke. He has taught me even more since his stroke about patience, the power of thoughts, determination, and willpower.

I have been blessed to have many wonderful colleagues who have helped me grow. The two who became my closest friends have encouraged me the most with writing this book, Donna Gard and Judy Pratt. Their knowledge and wisdom (and Donna's suggestions) have been priceless.

I have been blessed to have great friends who taught me a lot about life: Katherine Kennedy (and her parents Larry and Patricia), Cindy Schroder, and Victoria, Kelly and Jim who have widened my vision by introducing out-of-the-ordinary classes to me or encouraged me to look at life with new vision.

My two childhood friends, Susie Matson and Lee Ann Weblemoe, have believed in me since I was in Kindergarten. They helped me grow and have showed up for me all of my life.

Ethel Lombardi, one of the 22 original Reiki Masters in the United States, is by far my favorite teacher. Her influence, as well as Drs. John and Marilyn Rosner from McGill University in Montreal (who started the International Institute of Integral Human Sciences), helped me develop my inner vision.

To all of my teammates (teachers I taught with), administrators (most especially Dr. Carolyn Heitz, our reading coordinator), and school district's that believed in me . . . thank you.

I would especially like to acknowledge Kari Carlson, my original editor. I thought I knew how to write quite well—I taught it long enough. Now I know why authors rely on professional editors—she gracefully taught me that I am a still a lifelong learner. Thank you!

This book is dedicated to all of my students over my 30 year span of teaching in public schools--you have been a gift.

Introduction

I now understand why Grandma Moses was in her 70's when she became a famous artist. She was a simple farmer's wife until her arthritis forced her into <u>painting</u> a Christmas present for the postman-- instead of making him one of her beautiful embroideries. One painting led to many more. At first, they sold for very little—now, they are valuable American Folk Art.

I'm almost seventy years old! Like Grandma Moses, it has taken me a long time to realize my potential. Maybe it's because I like who I am now (that was not always the case over the years). I remember wishing I could be someone famous, or rich, or something other than what I was. Now, I wouldn't trade my experiences, both the good and the ugly, for anything. It has taken me a long time to come to peace with why I took the roads I did in life.

What makes me laugh the most at my past self is the amount of things I learned wrong in life. Probably the first of my mistaken learning's was thinking Abraham Lincoln was Jesus Christ. I'm serious! At Five years old, I was given a Christmas present of a picture of Jesus by my Sunday school teacher. This picture did not match the picture of 'Him' in the stained glass dome of our church that I stared at every Sunday while laying on my mom's lap.

At some point I decided Abraham Lincoln was pictured in the center of the dome because this church is in Lincoln, Nebraska. Wrong conclusion! I did not learn, until a few years ago, that Abraham Lincoln was in the center of the dome because the church founders had started a university first. They chose a mortal for the dome so the college students would have a "human model" for inspiration. If Lincoln could leave his mark on the growth of a nation, their student's could make a positive difference in their own world.

So here I am, still uncovering "new" information about life in general. I can tell you I do miss seeing Abraham Lincoln's picture in that stained glass dome. It's still there, but I'm not. I recently heard Daniel Day Lewis talking about his role as Abraham Lincoln in a movie. Mr. Lewis stayed 'in character' for the entire filming and he said in an interview about Lincoln, "I still miss him." I understand.

I ended up getting my college degree from this same college, Nebraska Wesleyan University. I wonder if those founding fathers, who chose Abraham Lincoln as an example, would be proud of my accomplishments over the years. There were days I basked in the warmth of pride. There were also days I fell short of my goals.

Now that I'm older, I'm grateful for the wisdom that has come with age and a wide variety of experiences. I appreciate the opportunities I've had over the years to learn and grow. I am a much better grandparent than I was a parent. I am a much better student than I was when I was in college. I am a much better teacher than I was 30 years ago. In fact, there isn't much that I haven't improved on over the years.

Thank goodness I've learned I'd rather be happy than right. I'd rather be who I am than someone else, I'd rather be kind than too stubborn to care, I'd rather be a work of art in progress than a finished painting. I'd rather be free to share what I've learned over the years than not share at all. Most of all, I'd rather "model ideas" for better tomorrows . . .

I call myself a lifelong learner and teacher, even though I'm retired from teaching. I haven't given up my vision for better tomorrows for all children—not just mine. Some of my teaching strategies are older than the hills, but they worked well and they still do.

I taught adolescents in four states. Each time I moved, I had exactly the training in the "new current thing" the school district was looking for to incorporate in their district. I taught long enough that some strategies we had used and abandoned for the next "new thing" came back around and were introduced as the "latest new thing" in education. When I was fund raising for schools in the fifth state I lived in—they were introducing the "newest" educational strategies I had used years and years ago.

The Nine Keys for Better Tomorrows (the subtitle) are mainly a composite of the educational strategies I used as a teacher in my classrooms; they helped me be a better parent and grandparent, too. From my experiences, these Keys are what can cause people to lose their pass code (feeling lost or incapable of achieving success and finding fulfillment in life).

1. **Listen**. Have you ever experienced not being heard? The first chapter answers the questions: What gets in the way of someone's capacity to listen to a child; what are the possible results? **We can change: Learn how to raise your listening intelligence.**

2. **Expand** your Perspective by adopting the "theory" everyone is a work of art in progress. **We can progress:** What do all humans need? **Learn how to build Self Confidence.**

3. **Knowing YOU matter** is a crucial Self Esteem need. How do you stop Invalidation; how do you validate yourself and others? Learn how to know for sure that YOU do matter to the people around you.

4. **Trust** what lies within you. You were born with innate preferences, are naturally smart in some area, and have a purpose. **Discover your own Self preferences; Uncover how you prefer to learn;** How **are you choosing to be?** Take a guess! Are you most like the first person on earth or the second or . . .

5. **Raise your natural awareness** about your innate talents and gifts in a fun way. Compare your birth date energy to nature's teachers energy—animals, fairy tale/folk lore characters, colors, planets. **Learn about the possible Plus, Minus and Interesting aspects of your inborn traits.**

6. Be **open to the coincidences** of your name legacy. **What do you know and what would you like to learn about the energy of your given name?** Are you more naturally a

communicator, an organizer or a peacemaker? **Learn how to stretch your mind through new ideas.**

7. **Remember** to Turn! Turn! Turn! **Learn about the 'Nine Year Cycle' Theory.** What grade are you in, personally, in this calendar year? **What could you do differently?**

8. **Educate** your Self before choosing your Next Steps. **How to strengthen your Energy (EMF), improve your thoughts, and guide your emotions.**

9. **Commit** to loving the child within you, so you can inspire the child in front of you. The importance of: environment, character development, and your relationship with yourself. Simple Positive Actions you can take and **how mankind eventually evolves.**

You can tell I look at life a little differently. Because I am a searcher for why things are the way they are, I have taken a wide variety of classes. These classes have introduced me to many 'outside the norm' ideas for a girl from the Midwest raised in a 'religious' community. Who starts an entire community (college, town, church, schools) to keep their kids away from sin city . . . which was Lincoln, Nebraska? Have you been to Lincoln? It isn't like Las Vegas!

How did I get to where I am now on my journey? It is the older civilizations on earth that have provided, for me, a unique perspective for learning about the human capacity for growth. Asia, Africa, and Europe have civilizations way older than the United States. Thankfully, I was able to retire early from teaching to uncover some of the unique perspectives that I have found invaluable. Consequently, when I talk about education, I don't mean just learning from inside the walls of a brick and mortar school.

Every parent I've met wants the possibility of better tomorrows—especially for their children and grandchildren. My parents lived through World War I, II and the great depression. My mom and dad (before the depression) went to college— only because they were the youngest and their older siblings could work the family farms. My parents believed in the value of education, so they built a house by a college. All six of their children could live at home, work, and pay for their own tuition. They gave us all the opportunity to **grow beyond them**.

My generation (in my family) inherited the same mentality— **to give our children the opportunity to evolve beyond us**. We also inherited my parents **'mindset': They believed every child should have an opportunity to expand his or her knowledge and develop skills to accomplish a reason for being or purpose**. My parents were adamant that their children's purpose better be a positive one for the next generation— their grandchildren. It's not a surprise that all six of their children were teachers!

I thought my parents were using this 'mindset' just to motivate six children!

Imagine my surprise when I read in a highly regarded book that,

"Everyone has a purpose, <u>or reason for being</u>, that fit into three very Broad Life Callings: to teach, lead, or heal."

These three broad life callings fit my generation of women. When I graduated from college, a woman's 'higher level' career choices were: to be a teacher, a nurse (healer) or an office manager (a leader). However, if you look at it from a broader perspective—teach, lead or heal—goes beyond gender, generations or any stereotypes.

How is that possible? I'm a <u>teacher</u> by profession, but a family friend is a janitor at a church; her broad life calling would also be classified as a teacher. She teaches people how to be responsible for a sacred space and *<u>models an idea</u>* that people can learn from. *A <u>teacher</u> models ideas for developmental growth.*

The President of the United States is a <u>leader</u>— so is every CEO, manager of an office, coach, and parent. A leader is someone in charge of guiding or directing others. *A <u>leader</u> makes decisions that affects others or <u>models an idea</u> others can follow.*

A doctor or a nurse is a <u>healer</u>, but so is the friend who hugs you when you have been hurt. *A healer can cure or treat illness or injuries*; **a** *healer can also __model an idea__ for making a difficult situation better* whether it is a health concern or a sad heart.

You have the choice to *teach, lead, or heal* in the positive, the negative, or not at all. *Consequently, you can be a leader for the children around you by not leading at all!* In some situations, that is not a bad thing. I would rather have someone choose to not lead at all instead of choosing to lead in a negative way. *You can be a negative healer by choosing to ignore a child who is hurt. You can be a positive teacher by choosing to teach your children how to be their best.*

I feel most people are a variety of a bunch of these combinations over a lifetime. I know I have been. What seems to be true is that every generation hopes the state of affairs on earth, especially in regards to their children, improves. My first year of teaching was in a farming community in Kansas. I still remember their mentality . . .

My fourth graders loved show and tell time because school was their 'socialization' time. Bobby would stand up and tell about his experience with helping to birth a new calf the night before. My mouth would be hanging open as he explained in detail how he had to pull and pull and finally yank the calf out. He was 10 years old. The rest of the kids would listen and shake their heads and say, "Yup, I had that happen." I won't even tell you what he had to do to his pigs. However, my student's always had the same reaction. "Yup, I had that happen."

It was as if everything was okay in their world when they had the same experience as everyone else. My parents wanted me to have better experiences; I want greater tomorrows for my child, my grandchildren and their children. News Flash. . . . the only constant seems to be change; all civilizations and environments change over time. Education is only part of the 'environment' equation. How you and I choose to BE with those beautiful babies that toddle into tomorrow is crucial for humanity's development. I have a theory. "Civilizations only become more evolved when the children they raise are taught to go beyond the previous generation's level of understanding— how about trying it without wars, abuse, or neglect?"

How did I begin searching for a broader vision of my possible future and come to peace with my past? I decided to start enjoying the journey.

Reading "<u>Grandma, I Lost the Pass Code to My Brain</u>" should be educational and fun. You get to learn more about your Self and the children you teach, lead or heal. By looking at your own and your children's choices from a different perspective AND by incorporating tried and true strategies, you learn to grow in a very interesting and child friendly way.

I know a secret about kids I'll share with you. Most of them love stories! My students always thought they were taking me off task by getting me to tell them a story. They never realized my 'stories' they loved hearing about (like some of the stories in this book) were a part of the most important lessons they could learn about life. Enjoy the journey!

Sow a thought, reap an act;
Sow an act, reap a habit;
Sow a habit, reap a character;
Sow a character, reap a destiny.

CHAPTER 1

The First Key for Better Tomorrows: Learn to Listen with Your Heart

My six-year-old granddaughter was not having a good day—she failed her math test at school and was in trouble at home. We were picking up the toy room together when she finally plopped down near me and the words came tumbling out of her mouth, "Grandma, I lost the pass code to my brain! I can't do anything right AND GOD IS NOT HELPING ME!"

I was stunned! How in the world would a six year old come up with a statement like that? She was dead serious and visibly upset. I quickly replied, "Oh, Honey, God is helping you! He gave you the ability to make choices. We can work together to remember it OR you can change the pass code anytime you want." Her face softened. She immediately wanted to know how. I continued, "So, if you could remember, what do you think your password would be?"

She quickly corrected me, "it's not a password, it's a pass code. It's all numbers." At this point, I was thinking "and she's having trouble with math?" Any differences between a pass <u>word</u> and a pass <u>code</u> had never occurred to me.

We started talking it out together. I asked her if the code was the numbers up to her age: 1, 2, 3, 4, 5, and 6? She shook her head no. I told her I was grateful it wasn't because I'd have to count a long time to get to my pass code! She laughed, relaxed, and started to think. She remembered it was 10 numbers. She rattled off 10 numbers a few times and finally said, "That's it!" A totally different, more confident child was sitting beside me.

> I asked my granddaughter why she used a pass code to open (access) her brain. She said, "Grandma, everyone knows a brain is like a computer, it stores everything you learn. Since Mom puts in letters and numbers to open her computer, I decided to use a secret pass code of numbers to open my brain because I don't like to spell words." (She really loves secret codes!)

Who but a child would express thoughts and feelings in such a remarkably unique way? **One of the greatest gifts children bring into our daily lives is the innocent and ingeniously candid expressions and actions they have to life situations.** I know for certain, after 30 years of teaching children, that my students (all under the age of 13) were also some of my best teachers. Because I paid attention and **listened with my heart** to my granddaughter, I was able to use my experience at the right time for her.

Do you have the time to pay attention and listen? I don't know about you, but my life can sure get out of control real fast. Even as an adult, I've lost touch with my sense of self—my identity, nature, character, and natural personality—more times than I can count. You would think it would get easier as I get older. Not really! Those life milestones and new opportunities still add up to more responsibility; it just looks different. As a grandma, I really like my granddaughter's idea of secret pass codes to access my brain. I'd have to write it down though!

In fact, my granddaughter is on the right track. A brain is like a computer because they are both as smart as the data they are fed (input) and as efficient as our ability to find what we've stored (output). My 90-year-old mother-in-law used to say her brain could only hold so much—at her age, some of the data was bound to fall out. Then she'd laugh—she got such a charge out of herself. Actually, brains do need charging! I'm at my best when I'm plugged into my own energy source: my body, mind (awareness), and spirit.

While my body's energy is re-energized by food, water, and oxygen, my mind feels recharged when I discover, learn, and create. My spirit (soul, heart, essence) is energized and more motivated by my own willpower to be and achieve (and laughter).

What would a disconnected (unplugged) brain be like? I can't think of a better example of a disconnected energy source than my husband's. Even though he's smart (he has a Master's degree in Education), he's had a few strokes. The thoughts are in his head, but he "short circuits" when trying to retrieve words—he has to have water and eat or his body's energy battery gets so low he simply can't talk. When he gets upset and can't access the right words, he then loses his will (spirit) to talk because of his frustration and anger at himself. He is good at recharging his mind—he has an unusual thirst for knowledge and is very curious.

My husband has the time, but he doesn't have the capacity to listen with his heart. From my experience with my students and husband, I realized my thoughts, emotions, and energy can interfere with my capacity to listen at all. My granddaughter calls it losing her pass code. I describe it as **a disconnect from my natural personality**. I feel more naturally myself when I'm feeling a certain sense of ease with who I am; I'm in a balanced state—my body, mind, and spirit are working in harmony, allowing me to be at my best.

Feeling a sense of ease within my Self is so important. After all, you and I are living on Earth, where it's possible to do much more than simply survive. When I'm feeling connected to my body, mind, and spirit, I create opportunities to feel fulfilled by who I am! Feeling fulfilled means I get to experience feeling complete, accomplished, satisfied, content, rewarded, happy...

Oh, what a feeling! Have you ever seen a child's face when he or she accomplishes a new task (like learning to ride a bike)? Watch a teacher or parent light up with the "Oh, I get it!" response from a child. Do you have a favorite sports team or enjoy the Olympics? As fans, you and I get to experience the thrill of success (fulfillment) or the agony of defeat. As a team's avid fan, you and I either learn how to celebrate success or learn how to hope for better tomorrows. Maybe the Chicago Cubs will win a World Series—that would be fulfilling for some.

You and I also have a right to **feel fulfilled with what we are choosing to do**. Maybe that's why, when we were children, we were often asked, "What do you want to do when you grow up?" Some people call our "future doings" a **Destiny (a reason for being).** However, I have a friend who works to make money so she can fulfill her destiny to volunteer. I think all Destinies have a secret purpose; they are a chance to teach those who follow in our footsteps. Life is a relay race—you and I pass on our knowledge and experiences to the next generation. Why? Two teachers I mentored 20 years ago are now my grandchildren's principals!

I feel our reason for being is also an opportunity for you and me to widen the circle of people we influence; it is a chance for us to BE, not just do. It is why **all our communities** (family, friends, jobs, churches, organizations, teams, countries, states, etc.) **fulfill needs:**

We are given an essential sense of belonging to something bigger than ourselves.

We are given life experiences to help us develop who we are.

We are given opportunities to feel fulfilled by being who we are while doing what makes us happy.

Learning, teaching, writing, sharing—these are the things I do that make me happy. Schools teach us skills and introduce us to a varied curriculum so we can discover what makes us happy. My daughter asked me and my husband when we knew we wanted to be teachers. We laughed. My answer was in college; his was after he'd been teaching for three months. We could change jobs if we weren't happy teaching because we'd had a good, broad education.

I wish every child's circumstances encouraged happy tomorrows. During the vulnerable stages of life from childhood to adulthood, other people's opinions, available role models, lack of finances or opportunities, disabilities, misfortunes, etc., can interrupt visions for happy tomorrows. It can be so disheartening to be limited by any of these circumstances.

I once taught a blind child. His vision for his better tomorrows (in sixth grade) was to become a rodeo clown! He knew who he was—a clown. He had that part right! He was funny, entertaining, engaging, and loved to tease people. His parents and I didn't think a rodeo, with big angry bulls chasing him, was the best place for a blind person to be. Obviously, he listened to us because he became a customer service representative for an insurance company. It was not an exciting career, which is why he wanted to work at a rodeo. When he lost his job, I think it was a good thing for him! He eventually got excited to try other possibilities and moved out west on his own to go to college. He improved his circumstances by listening to his own heart and gave himself new avenues to find happiness. He was not as limited by his disability.

My blind student's parents and I just wanted him to have the opportunity to grow beyond our generation. It wasn't that long ago that he would not have been allowed in a public school. He started his sixth grade year using a noisy Braille six key machine. Besides the fact it was very disruptive to his classmates, I had to learn Braille One. I enjoyed learning Braille, but I think the seven teachers he had the next year would not have appreciated the time it took.

With help, I was able to get him on a Braille and Speak, which is a computer with a Braille keyboard that verbally repeated what he wrote and printed his work out in English. This one piece of technology took away a big limitation, and then he could succeed in high school or college or a variety of careers— if he wanted to—on his own.

Don't you want that kind of attention for your child? I do! My daughter, at four years old, sat on her uncle's lap (on his newspaper) and grabbed his face in her little hands. She said, "Uncle Rex, look at me! I'm talking to you." She just wanted to be listened to from **his** heart.

He was so shocked by his preoccupation with his own thoughts that he ended up writing a sermon. As a minister, he knew this was his sign to inspire his congregation to **fulfill their responsibilities to the children in their lives**. It was a "What Would Jesus Do" sermon.

Think about the history of mankind. The first humans were lucky to survive. The surviving generations began to live in small groups and developed inspiring stories—cultural lore, fables, myths, etc. — for a purpose: **to civilize (educate and develop) future generations**.

I was born before TVs or computers were available. I was 10 when I started watching the world news on TV, and it expanded my world! A mere 12 years later, I had students from five of the seven continents in my classroom. (I knew something about where they had lived because of TV.) I remember thinking, *"my classroom is a miniature copy of the big world!"*

I had a few students in that class who had emigrated from Third-world countries. These kids had given up talking because they'd never been heard at all. Like my husband, who'd lost his will to talk, they were frustrated and apathetic. I learned that year the difference just listening to a child can make. **It's crucial for a child's developmental growth!**

I eventually grew to see all life on Earth as THE BIG SCHOOL and decided **each and every one of us is both a student and a teacher.** When I viewed my life's "growing up" experiences as opportunities to learn and grow, the only way I failed was if I failed to learn from those experiences. If you and I learn well from our experiences, WE can become people who evolve and bring hope to the still-hopeless on Earth—those who give up thinking about their tomorrows because of a sometimes thoughtless mankind.

It was not always about how quickly I learned, but how thoroughly I became prepared. Unless I use what I've been taught, that data can fly way out of my pass code range. From my experience, **thought management and emotional awareness are essential preparation requirements for our future!** Improving our thoughts, words, and deeds gives us a wider variety of choice and greater hope for better tomorrows. In my classroom, a preparation requirement for developmental growth was to start the year with a conversation.

I taught sixth grade for many years. If you're familiar with that age, budding hormones can get in the way of the learning process. So my teammates and I "set the stage," telling our students about the opportunities they could have in the next six to eight years: they could drive, have a job, own a car, apply for college or job training programs, they could get married and even have a child. How they developed their skills today would affect those tomorrows.

The parents of our students panicked! We had to remind them of **the purpose of parenthood: to prepare your children for adulthood.**

How well you and I teach our children often depends on how well we **listened** to what we were taught! *What if you were not taught all you needed to know?* I'm familiar with school curricula and there are some gaps in the skills being taught. For example, we taught higher-order thinking skills, but teaching a child how to think in the first place was considered the parents' responsibility. Do schools teach how to manage emotions? The guidance counselor talked about the wide variety of emotions available and the importance of choosing well because emotions affect our actions and interactions. Emotional Intelligence is a bit more involved.

For me, learning well from **my own experiences** has been my greatest resource for encouraging better tomorrows for my students. For example, I had a sixth grade student who was in reading recovery. I discovered his thoughts of himself during our first conference. He was bemoaning the fact he had extra reading because he was too stupid to catch on. WHOA! Did I hear him right? I asked him if he thought he was dumb.

He said, "Duh! I'm in the dummy reading class."

I told him he was in the reading recovery class—designed for kids who were less than two years below grade level—because we knew he was smart. We felt he could recover the reading skills he missed. Either he was absent when some of the skills were taught or he had not had the opportunity to use the skills enough. **It could be he just wasn't ready to listen when the skills were taught.** *I wish you could have seen him processing this information.*

He was shocked, "You mean I'm not dumb?"

I replied, "How could you possibly think you are dumb?" I continued, "Look at you-- you are a very gifted athlete, you're socially witty and clever, you know how to ask thoughtful questions, you get along with well a wide variety of people, and, most importantly, you're very capable of learning any skill."

His brain was now totally in the "on" position! This child was dramatically different, in a great way, by the end of the year. At that first conference, I asked him to use the same techniques he had used to become athletically smart and apply them to reading. He had to listen to what the teacher (coach) was teaching him, practice the skills every day (just like he did his quarterback skills at football practice), and use a variety of them in other subjects (just like he used his quarterback skills in more than just one football game.)

That day, this child remembered the pass code to his brain. It changed his whole perception of who he was and what he thought he was capable of learning. This is an example of how thoughts and emotions get in the way of words and deeds. He thought he was dumb, his emotional 'talk' was destructive, and he was not engaged in learning.

How did I know this one thought—"I'm dumb"—was holding him back? *Experience.* I was told by a guidance counselor I was not smart enough to go to college! My dad, a school administrator, always took the side of the teacher, but not this time. I had to retake the college entrance exam when I was well rested. I had a much higher score and started believing that I was smarter than the counselor thought. I went to college and earned a Bachelor of Arts degree in Education. I took more classes and now have a Master's Equivalency focusing on at-risk children. How lucky I was to have my dad stand up for me. I would not be where I am today had he not!

A generation later, my daughter was told that her kindergarten child was not participating in class. They rated her time on task and she was involved in learning only 60% of the time. Since her brother and dad have Attention Deficit Disorder, the first thought was: is she ADD?

My daughter's experience taught her to help her daughter by modeling an idea. She asked her daughter why she didn't participate in lessons like "Jolly Phonics"? She said, "Mom, I'm tired after recess, and I like watching everyone else." My daughter quickly replied, "You don't have a choice—it is not an option to sit and watch." Her time on task improved; her mom had wisely asked the right question.

A low point in my life was being told I wasn't smart enough for college, but the right person was there for me. He was not just smart; **he listened** with his heart and was **experience wise**! I try to "pay it forward." Fortunately, you have the ability to help others as I was helped. Unfortunately, like my guidance counselor, you can choose to be negative. Even though I had a B average, she inferred I wasn't capable based on one test. She taught me how NOT to be.

I would much rather be like my dad, who believed I was capable, or my daughter, who taught his great-granddaughter how to be capable. My parents would be thrilled their grandchild is honoring their generational mentality and mindset to achieve better tomorrows.

The right person for your **parental development growth**, as an adult, is you. Think of yourself as a beautifully innocent and remarkable child! (Personally, I think that's why my youngest grandchild looks like I did as a child—to remind me of who I was then.)

I don't judge my youngest grandchild or compare her to other children, or expect her to do things she hasn't learned yet. I love her just the way she is—unique and one of a kind. I see her as a beautiful child with her own exceptional talents and gifts. She is a work of art in progress. I just want her to be happy with who she is and capable of finding her great potential for her own better tomorrows.

So, why do I sometimes judge myself so harshly or compare myself to those around me? Why do I sometimes think *"What did I do wrong?"* when a person is standoffish or mad? What am I choosing to tell myself? I ended up asking myself an important question: "Lois, when was the last time you talked to yourself with the compassion you feel when you talk to your youngest grandchild?"

The highest form of love is compassion. Give to yourself what you would want your children to be given. Give to your children the wisdom you gained from those who taught you how to be the best you can be. YOU are exactly the right person to plant the seeds for better tomorrows in yourself and in your children. Start with paying attention to what you are saying to the people around you and **to what you are telling yourself.**

How to Raise Your "Listening from the Heart" Intelligence.

1. To change how you listen, change how you think! When I read Plato's quote, "Thinking is the talking of the soul with itself," I decided to choose different thoughts. Why? I chose to change my thoughts because my current way of thinking was altering my awareness of myself and my own thoughts were interfering with how I was listening to children. I was letting other people's thoughts and opinions override my own.

How did I accomplish changing my thoughts?

I took a self improvement class. An exercise that really affected me in this class was to first stand in front of a classmate and say something nice to her. I said, "Oh, you look so cute today." Second, I was to step back and say "critical opinion thoughts". I stepped back and said out loud, "Where did you get that ugly sweater, your hair is a joke, and I really hate those ridiculous looking shoes."

While everyone laughed at first, it soon became obvious the second step of this process was very harmful to everyone in the class. How? Those second set of thoughts were opinions based on my own preferences and didn't allow for the other person's individuality. I never even heard her say "thank you" to the first compliment because my runaway critical thoughts kept going even after I was done speaking out loud. Those "mind thoughts" took away my ability to LISTEN! How many times have you **not** heard someone say something to you because your brain was on negative thought overload?

To increase your Child Listening Intelligence, STOP your thought frenzy. How can you help your misbehaving child improve when you go on thought frenzies? "You always forget your homework" or "You never listen to directions . . . blah, blah, blah!" When your child misbehaves, you can choose to change a negative situation into a positive opening for a conversation! How about trying "Usually you're responsible, is there a reason you're choosing not to be?" or "This behavior is unlike you, is there something bothering you?" or "Let's both take a time out and then we will discuss it." This strategy gives you both a chance to slow down, think, AND get rid of the frenzies and mind clutter. It gives you an opportunity to think better thoughts about your child and it encourages your child to reconnect to his or her own natural sense of Self.

I have read that Ralph Waldo Emerson believed "The soul of God is poured into the world through the thoughts of man." Thinking back, after my first class, I realized my poorest thoughts were at a time when I had lost my faith. I, like my granddaughter, thought God (my personal higher power) was not helping me. I lost my confidence, was disillusioned, and ill at ease. So, I took another class!

In this class, I learned **how to cancel thoughts**. The theory is as follows.

> *It takes 30 seconds before a thought becomes permanently recorded in your brain. If you think a thought you don't want, you simply immediately say, "cancel, cancel, cancel," (silently or out loud) and the thought will not be permanently recorded in your memory.*

I'm not kidding! Even though it seems too simple to work, I can tell you from my experience that it does. One of my friends, a single parent, liked the changes in me after I tried this theory. She decided to try the cancel theory to get rid of her unhealthy thoughts for two weeks. She asked her daughter to help her catch the negative, opinionated, judgmental, untrue thoughts. Not only did it work for her, her daughter improved her thoughts, too! Like me, they both still use this technique!

I taught my granddaughter this method of canceling out thoughts. She is a gifted visual learner and sees things I don't even notice. Fortunately, at eight years old, she's sensitive to people's actions and reactions. Unfortunately, she assumes she's always at fault when someone gets mad or sad. I asked her to **"cancel, cancel, cancel"** that thought and replace it with **"People are responsible for choosing their own thoughts and emotions."** Shortly thereafter, I heard her say out loud to herself, "I'm stupid." Then I heard a "cancel, cancel, cancel." I love it when that happens because it means she's listening with her heart to the child within herself! She's her own positive best friend.

2. Improve your thoughts and listening by choosing a bigger picture mentality. I was once molested as a child. What is the bigger picture mentality in this situation? My counseling sessions and personal experience helped me identify signs of abuse in a few of my students. I was able to ask good questions, listen, and get them help. The abusive adults were removed from the homes. Helping these children was the silver lining in the cloud of my hard experience.

This is why I'm attached to the concept that there could be a soul of a higher power—a ray of light at the end of the sometimes dark tunnel of life experiences—that guides everyone toward greater ideals. If I choose to strengthen my character by learning from a negative situation, I can share my story with others. Wouldn't you help your neighbors by telling them to lock their doors after your home was robbed? That's bigger picture mentality.

3. Clear away your own mind clutter daily! Another strategy I use came to me when I was erasing the board at the end of the day. I erased all the stuff I wrote on the board at the end of each day so I was ready for a new day. I decided to do that with my thoughts. At night, I mentally erased any negative thoughts I had that were harmful to me or to a child. In the morning, I was a clean slate! Any child I had to discipline the day before got a clean slate each day, too! Using a clean slate mentality erased harmful words like "you always" or "you never" from my vocabulary.

4. Review your emotions and choose when to hold on to an emotion or when to fold one. Since thoughts create emotions, I also review my emotions periodically. Human emotions are like a double-edged sword: they are both a gift and a test. For me, the test was to realize I have the power to change my emotions. YOU also have the ability to choose. Do you hold on to unhealthy emotions? Do you let go of an emotion that no longer suits you?

Why would I continue to hold on to an emotion that makes me sad or mad, especially if it happened years ago? I've had some unnerving experiences that kept me from enjoying who I am until I chose to let the emotion go. For example, when my dad passed away, I was devastated. One day, shortly after he passed, I found myself driving aimlessly around town because I had seen a burial vault on the truck next to me. Twenty minutes had gone by and I was late getting home to my child. Not healthy.

I decided to think I *was* lucky to have a wonderful dad and *am* lucky to be a mom. So, I choose to honor my dad every year by mentally talking with him on his birthday. I thank him for what he taught me that I can now teach my child. I tell him about my accomplishments and share my dreams for the next year with him. Taking time to "talk with Dad" reminds me of the greater possibilities within me because of his influence.

5. Choose to guide your daily emotions. I learned from the Reiki Principles (an Eastern healing art) to say:

JUST FOR TODAY, DO NOT WORRY. (Worry puts you in the future "what if").

JUST FOR TODAY, DO NOT ANGER. (Anger puts you in the past "why me").

Both worry and anger cause thought frenzy that can short circuit your capacity to <u>think</u> and <u>listen well</u>. I have these principles framed on the wall by the door so I say them when I leave home. I've grown accustomed to repeating them to myself, especially when my muscles feel tight or my jaw hurts—my signs that I'm worrying or angry!

6. ASK FOR HELP. If I have a problem I can't seem to find a solution to, I ask my higher power for help. Invariably, I get an answer. For really important questions that affect other people, I also ask for three signs that I'm on the right track. I didn't think this up on my own! One of my Native American friends taught me to ask for signs using earthly messengers, too.

How have my signs appeared? I might see an animal that means something to me, hear a song that answers my question, or watch a TV show about the topic, or run into a person who— out of the blue— unknowingly answers my question. I also have positive affirmation card sets (angel cards and animal cards) around my house that often lead me to the answer when I pull a card. I say a prayer of gratitude before going to sleep and often wake up with insights to nagging situations. These ideas usually expand my perspective and strengthen my sense of ease.

Realize You Have Two Ears and One Mouth for a Reason

While all of these strategies will help you connect to your *own* pass code or natural personality (Self), they will also expand your ability to pay attention to a child in a more heartfelt, meaningful way. A clear body, mind, and spirit allows you to make the most of the time you have to listen. You also get to listen with your heart to the childlike spirit within you that is so much wiser than you know. You become a present (everyday) to yourself and the children around you.

> **"Yesterday's experience is Today's insight for creating better Tomorrows."**
>
> Lois Hinkly

CHAPTER 2

The Second Key for Better Tomorrows: Expand Your Perspective

What if you thought of yourself and those around you as a work of art in progress? I would never have thought of people as a work of art until I started teaching and a friend (with eight children) said,

> *"If you ever teach my children, I expect you to look at them as a work of art, like a blank canvas or piece of clay. Each time you interact with them, build them up! Any time you leave a negative impression, it takes much longer to fill in and smooth out the hole you have made."*
> **Emmett Dennis**

I think every being on this planet is an extraordinary creation, like a work of art. I taught the reproductive system (sex education) for 25 years. Over the years, I grew to be in absolute awe of how life is conceived, developed, and born into this world. To fertilize an egg, the conditions have to be just right and the odds are really against us. If you'd seen those reproduction movies as much as I did, (especially the new ones) you'd agree. There is no question in my mind that every child created is a work of art.

Taking a work of art (like a child) and making it a masterpiece is a step-by-step process. That is why the words "in progress" are important. Synonyms for progress are advancement, growth, and/or improvement. For me, raising a child was like taking two steps forward and one step back over and over again. The backward steps were usually caused by interaction with others.

As a teacher, one of my favorite subjects to teach was science because words like "hypothesis", "probable", and "theory" do not leave a negative impression. The word "judge" can, especially for a child. One year, on the second day of class, a student told me I was weird. Most people consider the word weird a negative judgment, but I replied with a thank you. Her eyes widened; she suddenly knew I would not judge her and she could be herself. I would build her up and accept her **even if she was "weird" sometimes**.

Oh, the beauty and power of words! When I taught astronomy, I had to be careful to use the word "theory" constantly, especially when teaching the Big Bang Theory. Most of our students had never heard of it (except the TV show). Some of our students thought the Big Bang Theory was contradictory to *"In the beginning, God created..."* from the Bible. By using the word "theory", I didn't tear down or sound as though I were judging my students' possible religious beliefs.

There are many scientific theories that can be startling to children, like the Snowflake Theory that no two snowflakes are alike. I investigated the research on snowflakes. It made sense to me, and so I choose to think you are the only one like you on earth. I'm not alone. I went to a class taught by my favorite teacher—Ethel Lombardi. A classmate asked Ethel if she could take over Ethel's classes when she retired. Ethel got upset at this particular question. She quickly and vociferously responded,

"How dare you rob the world of you?! I'm the only one who can teach like me. You have people waiting to learn from you."

You talk about a wakeup call. If someone is waiting to learn from me, I'd better have my act together. (What is my pass code again?) Who is waiting for **you**? Pretty much everyone you meet! From the moment you are born, the people in your life have an opportunity to help you develop who you choose to become. It took me years to understand the beauty of this way of thinking—I get to learn and grow so I can be available to help others reach their potential.

In the past, young children were molded by a small group—parents, siblings, grandparents, a tribe, or a village. Not so much, now. Our world has grown to over seven billion people and the children of today interact with and are affected by far more people. Everyone has inherited an opportunity and responsibility to help the next generation develop. **Your words and your actions matter,** especially to the parents of the children who cross your path!

For example: At the time I was born, the leader of my country—the United States of America—was President Harry S. Truman. President Truman had just bombed Japan to end World War II. Can you imagine having to make that kind of decision as a leader? That's a heavy call to duty and a huge responsibility.

When I was older I discovered my birth certificate, instead of Central Time, had WAR TIME on it. (Who wants "War Time" on their birth certificate?) I started thinking—what if President Truman had made the decision to NOT use nuclear bombs on Hiroshima and Nagasaki to end the war? What if England and the United States had not become friends and allies to defeat Germany and Italy? My life would be completely different today, and so would yours! Truman's decision was crucial to every child brought into this world after 1945.

Your decisions and how you decide to be or NOT be is extremely important to the people around you—especially children. While we equate the word "child" with the next generation, a child is not just a human between birth and puberty. A child can be anyone incapable of being responsible for his or her own actions. That "child" could be an adult with Alzheimer's, Down's syndrome, or anyone who has to rely on someone else to help them reach their level of potential each day!

They say it takes a village to raise a child, yet the world has become our village. Suddenly, words and actions from people thousands of miles away can reach out and affect everyone—including people I love.

What if **all** world leaders chose to come from an **Encourage Positive Progress Perspective**? Oh, the places we could go as a civilization.

One of the biggest changes for me, and probably you, is the incredible progress of technology. We have 24 hour news services, sometimes inaccurate or biased, and we are bombarded by social networks and news from around the globe. If a catastrophe happens or a critical decision is made by a leader, it is instant news. How do children process all this data and how do they do it well? The value of adults in a child's life has expanded way beyond the scope of the original meaning of adult (not just a grown up, but a mature, experienced adult).

What has <u>not</u> changed in almost every country, culture, and religion on Earth is the <u>GOLDEN RULE</u>.
This is an essential rule of conduct that advises people to <u>TREAT OTHERS AS YOU WOULD LIKE TO BE TREATED YOURSELF.</u>

Unfortunately, some of mankind's leaders (like Japan's, Germany's and Italy's during WWII) decided that the end justifies the means. In other words, if you get your way, what does it matter if you harm someone else? *Ask the millions of people who lost loved ones in WWII.* This Machiavellian way of thought is described (in a dictionary) as amoral, unethical, dishonorable, and unprincipled.

Fortunately, we have many human beings focusing on further developing the civilization of mankind with grace. When you become a parent, teacher or leader for children, you have both an opportunity for growth and a responsibility. All of a sudden, who you were and what happened to you way back when was just a chance to learn from your experience to help others. Now, you get to use that experience to guide someone else in choosing how to be or not be.

As you walk down your life path with the children in your life, you can learn how to **walk softly in your own shoes**. What does that mean? When my friend Judy Pratt came up with "walk softly in your own shoes," we were discussing a person who had not yet shed emotions from her past that were negatively affecting her present actions and reactions. Immediately, I thought of a butterfly! Huh? Humans go through stages similar to other species; it just isn't as obvious as a caterpillar that morphs into a butterfly. The person we were discussing hadn't yet realized **she didn't have to be the same as she's always been**.

One of my students once asked me if I thought a caterpillar knew it was going to transform into a butterfly. I quickly replied, "I don't know, but I do know you get to change into something as beautiful." All of us can by choosing to walk a little softer in our own shoes.

I've learned to walk softer in my own shoes as a grandma because I'm using the wisdom I've gained from my experience! With the availability of technology, I want to reach out to my grandchildren and guide them in a meaningful way. I can be a translator for them as they sift through the tremendous amount of data coming at them in this world. I get to guide how they look at things, so the way they interpret events helps them grow. **I am a storyteller** who can add wisdom and common sense to their perceptions.

> For two years I was lucky enough to teach Native American cultures. I gained a great deal of respect for these indigenous tribes. It was usually the grandparents or elders who taught the young children the skills they needed to survive. These **grandparents or elders were the children's storytellers—their words and actions taught a way of life.**

It's not as simple now. Let's go back to the theory that you are the only one like you on Earth. Have you begun to wonder: *"If I'm the only one like me, how come some of my family members have similar traits?"* Genetics! Just as you inherit physical characteristics like eye color, you inherit character traits.

However, your children also copy how you act and react. My daughter and my niece react to situations the same way a lot. My niece is adopted and biracial, my daughter is not. How could they be so similar? My brother and I were like two peas in a pod. My daughter copied me and his daughter copied him. Nowadays, would they mimic a movie star instead of us? That could be good or not so good! Our society is certainly not as self-contained as the indigenous tribes were, nor is it as self-contained as it was when you were a child.

Because our world has expanded, our children are exposed to a wider variety of people and situations. They are more vulnerable to ideas they may not be ready to absorb—through video games, TV, movies, internet sites, etc. Children who have adults helping them gain perspective may not be as affected by those outside influences.

Truthfully, **what a child needs most is LOVE and a sense of belonging!** The very first memory I have was of watching my family from my room. I was supposed to be sleeping, but I wanted nothing more than to be with them (I wanted to belong). I was four. Interestingly, some northwestern indigenous tribes did not name a child until he or she was four—when they felt the spirit entered the child's earthly body. What I have noticed with my tribe (family) is that age four is when my grandchildren hungered more for their independence; yet they still needed their 'family love' safety net at the end of the day.

I have been amazed at some of the coincidences I've stumbled on during my life journey. When I was teaching, I attended a workshop on the effects of birth order in a family. **The theory is each child in a family chooses actions for the sole purpose of getting their parents' love.** It follows that if the second child is the same sex as the first child in a family, the second child will choose the opposite behavior of the first one to separate themselves from their sibling and get their own attention and love.

This theory was true for our family. The oldest, a boy, was very responsible and the second boy was a trouble maker. The third child, a girl, was the caretaker. The fourth child, a boy, was a loner. The fifth, a boy, was the charmer.

The sixth, a girl, became the family clown. I was that family clown—it was the only way I got attention, and I didn't care if it was good or not so good attention. When I became a parent and my parents died, my clown side subsided.

What about blended families? How confusing is it for a child who lives half the time with one parent and half the time with the other parent and half siblings are involved? **As a parent in a blended family, you can shed your cocoon to help everyone to fly.** My biological grandchildren have my family, my first husband's family, and my current husband's family. They have their dad's birth mother, her family, and the family who adopted their dad. All that love and attention helps.

Whether you agree with this birth order theory doesn't matter. What is true for sure? **The main focus of a baby or small child is to get love and attention—either in a positive, neutral, or negative way.** When a child feels unloved, a disease or dysfunction with who he or she is can surface, kind of like losing the pass code to the brain. Whether you are a child or adult, basic human needs must be met in order to reach goals like self-actualization or self-fulfillment.

As a teacher, I attended a workshop on Maslow's theory of the five basic human needs. I agree with the theory; in fact, it was like finding a missing piece to a puzzle for me.

<u>Psychologist Abraham Maslow's Five Basic Human Needs</u>
Physiological needs (hunger, thirst)
Safety needs
Love and belonging needs
Esteem needs (Feeling valued)
Self-actualization/self-fulfillment needs

According to Maslow, we cannot approach a particular need until a previous one is satisfied. I cannot get to self-actualization if I don't have love and a sense of belonging. While the first two needs are pure common sense, the last three needs are colored by an individual's **self perception**. A child may be loved, but may not always feel the love. How can you feel valued by a family if (for some reason) you don't feel like you belong in the family? More importantly, it's close to impossible to build self esteem if a child doesn't feel safe. I've seen the results an unsafe situation can have on a child's self esteem and self confidence.

I was so lucky, as a sixth grade teacher, to be trained by Quest International. They offered two wonderfully written programs called "Skills for Growing" and "Skills for Adolescence." A cornerstone of the Skills for Adolescence program we used with our sixth graders was the Three-Legged Stool of Self Confidence. Their theory is that self confidence comes from feeling: 1. Lovable, 2. Capable, and 3. Responsible.

Feeling "short" in any of these three legs of self confidence can cause you to fall. The result—you can be thrown back to "survival mode." If I'm in survival mode, I am certainly out of touch with my natural personality. In fact, it is ultimately harmful.

One of my principals said, "The only difference between a child and an adult is age and experience." My daughter lost her dad when she was 10. Shortly thereafter, a friend of mine lost his dad. He finally said to me, "Your daughter helped me realize if she can survive the loss of her dad when she was 10 years old, I can survive losing mine at 40!" She's used her experience to help several people recover from family loss survival mode.

In fact, she helped her own family. At 10 years old, she asked me what song they were playing at her dad's funeral. I told her it was the Battle Hymn of the Republic. She looked at me incredulously and said, "But Mom, Dad was a Democrat!"

Her grandparents couldn't stop quietly chuckling over her remark! She innocently showed her dad's parents, who had just lost a son, how to walk softer in their own shoes in the worst of times. **Choosing to stay stuck in past traumatic life events is like a caterpillar refusing to become a butterfly. You are surviving life instead of rising above it.**

You increase your self confidence when you feel lovable, capable, and responsible. How can you feel good about yourself if you feel unloved and misbehave to get attention? What if you feel incapable and you manipulate others to get what you want? What if you feel irresponsible and competitively undermine someone else to get what you need? If you feel unloved, incapable, or irresponsible, how will it affect your personality/character?

I was once asked in a job interview, "What is the single most important quality in a good teacher?" The answer was, "A good personality." I think **a good personality means you are exhibiting a sense of ease with life**. Luckily, we have had many great personalities living on our planet. William Shakespeare is one who asked, "To be or not to be: that is the question. Whether 'tis nobler in the mind to suffer the slings and arrows of outrageous fortunes..."

Most species either fight or take flight when outrageous fortunes come their way. The species *Homo sapiens* (you are one) have more choices because our brains are more complex. When life gets hard—a loved one dies, a flood destroys your home, a hurricane or earthquake turns your life upside down—life changes. These times try our souls, but they are circumstances that can teach us how to overcome adversities. A child in this kind of survival mode is very vulnerable. Forget reaching self realization if a child does not have someone to guide them through "the slings and arrows of outrageous fortunes"!

What about the human-induced kind of outrageous fortunes? *One year, I had a student who had no morals or ethics. He would hit others for no reason; he would trip another child for fun. He had no boundaries and no fear of discipline. To me, it was apparent he had not felt loved or nurtured. In fact, the opposite was true—he had been abused. He took his shirt off one day on the playground and his back was full of little round scars. I asked him what happened and he told me his mother used to put her cigarettes out on his bare back when he was a baby. I nearly cried. I couldn't hide my horror or the compassion I felt for him.*

As a teacher and mandatory court reporter, I reported it to my principal. The child told me his mom had been declared "fit" by the courts. He was right. He also told me not to worry—he was taller than his mom now and he could take care of himself! **This child's behavior was a result of not feeling loved or safe; he was exactly the kind of child who is in danger of being in <u>permanent survival mode</u> AND of choosing a life of crime.**

*I was horrified that this had happened to this innocent child, and I was not able to make it better. Thankfully, I went to a conference shortly thereafter; the speaker talked about this kind of situation—**not being able to reach a child. He said, "Even Jesus Christ only got 11 out of 12!"** All I could do was to find ways to like him, so he could maybe choose to make some better choices.*

This incident changed my whole way of approaching students at the beginning of the school year. I became more watchful for past events that could affect a child's ability to learn. **I had already decided each child I taught deserved to be liked by me.** It doesn't take a rocket scientist to realize the difference being liked makes; it doesn't take a genius to realize how children retain what you teach-- Practice, practice!

Practice? That might be why someone who is older can be quite childlike with their words and deeds. My husband, after his stroke, had to relearn to walk, talk, and use his right arm again. He was a school principal, yet he became childlike. Therapy, practice, positive thoughts and a strong will were his keys; his slate had been wiped clean and he had to be retaught. By the way, his hole in one in golf was after his stroke—he really practiced well.

Can looking at the people around you as a piece of clay (a work of art in progress) help you be a better parent or teacher or leader? It can, especially if you **start with yourself**! Looking at myself as a work of art in progress helped me understand I had learned some things wrong. It comforted me as I healed events from my past that threw me into survival mode from time to time. I realized the negative situations had taught me how NOT to be.

If you look back through your childhood, there were probably some people who taught you how not to be. I became a teacher because I had several teachers that taught me how not to be; in fact, I pretty much didn't like school. I got in trouble for talking a lot and was once shut in a closet during my high school speech class for talking too much! How embarrassing and how ironic! I mean, aren't you suppose to talk in speech class? Truthfully, I was practicing speech wrong. However, the "shut in the closet" and "not smart enough" incidents made me more aware of my reactions with my students.

For example: *I had a student, a boy, who came in from recess holding his "funny bone" at the elbow. He said, "Oh, my UTERUS is killing me." Oops! We had just taught the skeletal and reproductive systems in science. He obviously meant his HUMERUS (upper arm bone) was hurting because he had hit it. He certainly had learned it wrong. My reaction to gently correct him instead of laughing was crucial for his friends to understand that any one of them could have made the same mistake. If I had made fun of him, you can bet he would have been teased (or possibly been called a girl or eventually bullied.)*

The "slings and arrows of outrageous fortunes" can help us grow, if we learn from those experiences. In fact, my past life lessons taught me to believe in a divine order. I wouldn't be where I am or who I am today without those experiences.

> I find it interesting that humans think of volcanoes and earthquakes as destructive forces. Scientifically, they are constructive forces. They actually end up building up the Earth! Is it possible to rethink that some of our past events that appear to leave destructive holes in our clay actually can eventually build us up constructively if we learn from them?

To NOT be is not always bad when it comes to words and deeds. Sometimes, not saying or doing something is a better choice. Choosing neutral during a heated discussion can be a wise course of action. Some of my daughter's wisest words to me when I was struggling with a problem were, "Mom, if you don't know what to do—don't do anything yet." Now, how did she get so smart?

Why do I wish I had somehow magically known all this when I was four years old and I buried my mother's wedding ring? My parents never found the ring. (In my defense, I was playing pirate.) The end result of my ring pirating was, the guilt left a hole in me wide enough to negatively color my thoughts of myself **for years**. My siblings, when they got in trouble, used to say, "Well, at least I didn't bury mom's wedding ring." More self guilt!

Thirty years later, I found a diamond ring on the first tee of a golf course. I turned it in at the club house. Some suggested I keep it, but that was not an option for me as I thought of my mom's ring. The next day, a lady came by my house with the ring on her finger. It was her mother's ring; her mom had just passed away. She gave me a hug and a card. She had slipped money in the card, but the knowledge of the ring's importance was way more valuable to me.

I immediately called my mom and told her I made up for burying her ring by finding another mother's ring. She said, "Oh, Honey, has that bothered you all these years? I should have never left it where you could reach it. Besides, you were always way more important to me than any ring!" All the guilt I had for years vanished!

My mother died three months later; however, the lessons she taught me live on in me, my child, and my grandchildren. I vowed, at four years old, to never take something that didn't belong to me again. I told every child I ever taught this story! **Parenting, teaching, and leading can be as simple as just sharing the wisdom you gained from childhood mistakes.**

YOU are a work of art in progress and you can be the artist that paints your own future. You can begin to heal the negative impression from your own past into wisdom for your future growth. When faced with a child who was abused by a parent or has lost the pass code to her brain, **it's important to expand your perspective about your own experiences.**

I find it interesting that some cultures put

a piece of coal in a Christmas

stocking if a child has been bad. A piece of coal under pressure

for a long time transforms into a diamond. Our life stories are

pearls of wisdom that we gained from the

good and not-so-good times in our life.

A pearl, by the way, starts out as a grain of sand that

irritated an oyster. Like a butterfly, the coal and grain of sand

go through stages to become what they are. So do you.

You are a work of art in progress and a valuable resource for

energizing the next generation toward better tomorrows.

How to Build Self Confidence

> **I was taught that every time I left a negative impression on someone else (or myself) it would take six positive impressions to fill in the whole I had made.**

What if you are leaving negative impressions on your own Self? The two biggest sources of natural light on our planet are the Sun (a star) and our Moon, which reflects the Sun's light at night. You, like the Sun, are the star in your life; your thoughts, words, and deeds are like the Moon—a reflection of who you are to the children in your life.

Like the Sun, I've had storms that generated negative self talk and some spots that caused me to listen to opinions that were not accurate. The reflection of negative self esteem can be harmful to the people you love the most. I don't know about you, but I lost my way as a parent when my own light was the lowest.

I started what I called **"The Shining Stars"** when **I noticed my grandchildren were leaving negative impression on each other.** After Thanksgiving, I told them they were like stars that could shine the best of their words and deeds on each other. For Christmas, a present from me was an opportunity to earn $5 so they could give a sibling (we drew names) a Christmas present. The kids were eleven, eight, six, and two years old at the time.

I had a Christmas tin filled with stars and gave each one of them a smaller tin box to put the stars they earned in. Once they earned a star, it could not be taken away. They would need 20 stars to get to $5. They could earn stars by being

  1. **Lovable,**   2. **Capable,**   and/or   3. **Responsible**.

I had a list of examples, too. They could show **they were Lovable** by taking good care of themselves, by being nice and kind toward one another, by showing appreciation, and by complimenting and caring for their family and friends. **Capable** meant they could finish tasks they started, learn a new skill, change a habit for the better (like pick up after themselves), follow directions, be a good role model for others, and be honest and patient with each other. **Responsible** meant that they could

27

be trusted to do chores and get homework done well and in a timely way, they could take turns gracefully, they could respect each others' space and belongings, and they could follow family or school rules.

We brainstormed some other examples until I felt they understood. They decided they could also tell Mom or Dad when someone should be given a star for a behavior they had appreciated receiving from a sister or brother.

What their parents and I were doing was catching them being good at something and focusing on that behavior instead of focusing on what they were doing wrong. At first, it took some teaching—you earned a star for helping your baby sister put on her shoes, etc. Eventually, it became contagious. Even the two year old caught on and figured out how to be a star. At one point she came up to me and started rubbing my feet because I do that for her to make her feel better.

The 11 year old, my step-grandson, lives with his half sisters every other week. Yet he managed, too! In fact, when it came time to take him shopping for his youngest sister, he was adorable. He said, "Grandma, I have $4.25 to shop for my baby sister. I went shopping and I think I found something she'd like for that amount of money." I said, "First of all, you were honest about how much money you have earned—that's another star. Then you planned and shopped ahead of time and were thoughtful about what she might like. You have earned your $5 for your baby sister."

The **Shining Stars were an opportunity to focus on giving to someone else** when the kids were writing their own wants list. After Christmas, I started to put the stars away and my daughter said, "No, Mom, we're keeping the stars out." She could really see a difference in their self confidence and in their behavior.

Children will do what they have to do to get your attention—whether it's positive or negative. Busy times for parents, like holidays, can bring negative attention-getting from kids. You could use daily stars, weekly charts, or even special notes on a bedtime pillow. It doesn't have to be money—earning extra alone time with a parent, grandparent, or friend can be a very special treat.

You can do Shining Stars for yourself with friends and family. My friends and I gave each other 10 little notes each Christmas for several years. When I'm feeling down, I reread them. **The notes remind me that I am lovable and capable of doing and saying things that make a positive difference for others.** When you take time to recharge your own self-confidence battery, like a star, you light the way for the ones you love to follow your lead.

CHAPTER 3

The Third Key for Better Tomorrows: Know That You Matter

What is matter? From a scientific perspective, matter is anything that has mass and takes up space. A star like our Sun has mass and takes up space; you have mass and take up space. You are born, you live, and you die, just like the sun is born, lives, and dies. Consequently, I like the concept that we are all children of the stars. **Every single living thing on this planet matters; every living thing gets a chance to shine!**

> Wait a minute. The Sun will die? Unfortunately, according to astronomers, our Sun will die. That is what stars eventually do. Fortunately, it will be approximately another four billion years until it does. Why do you think astronomers keep looking for Earth-like planets? Humans will have to find another Earth and figure out a way to move everyone to that planet, figure out how to move our Earth to a compatible star, or something else. Who knows? It is a really good reason for Earth's civilizations to press onward and upward in our development.

Since our Sun is classified as a middle-aged star, do you wonder if it's starting to feel kind of old? I read on the internet the other day that the Sun had an unusual hole; is it an age spot? Our Earth is middle-aged, too; do you think "Mother Earth" is feeling over the hill and starting to cleanse her own face? After all, many people start worrying about aging in the middle-aged years—when turning 40 or 50 years old. I couldn't wait to turn 16, 18, or 21, yet turning 40 wasn't as exciting. How are you going to feel when you turn 80, 90, or 100? It is possible you will live that long!

I asked my sister-in-law how it felt to be 90 years old. She said, "It was a long time coming, but I kind of expected it!" I'd never heard an age question answered so adorably and wisely. My sister-in-law is a nun who taught for 50 years. Nuns generally live 7 to 10 years longer than non-nuns. Why? Their optimism and attitude of gratitude! **They expect to age and appreciate the opportunity.** Aging just is; it's what humans do.

There are multiple definitions of the word "matter". There is matter as a noun, like I just talked about—something that has mass and takes up space. "There is also matter as a verb—saying that something **matters** is saying that it is important and has value. As people, we are already one definition—we have mass and take up space—but we can lose sight of the fact that people aren't just made of matter, they DO matter!" You, like the Sun, aren't just taking up space; **you matter**, you have value, and you get to shine no matter how old you are.

I remember sitting in the warm summer grass staring at the night sky watching the hundreds of stars twinkling above me as a child. I felt so tiny. Then, on Saturday mornings, I would watch the Mickey Mouse Club Show with Annette and Bobby and again I felt so small and unimportant. I remember comparing myself to the stars—both the astronomical ones and the Disney ones—and usually felt like I was insignificant as a child. I didn't yet understand that I just really wanted to shine or stand out in some way. How many children do you think feel the way I felt? Do you sometimes feel small—especially as you get older?

Feeling like you matter or are of value is a crucial self esteem need at any age. I identified with those feelings once again when I retired. I retired from teaching when I was 55 and moved to a warmer weather climate in Las Vegas. I had to work to pay for my health insurance and was hired by a friend to raise funds for schools. I was valued and felt for sure that I still mattered. Then my friend transferred to another city. My new boss did not value me; she actually chose to invalidate me until I had no choice but to resign.

Invalidate? I had an opportunity to take a class on validation/invalidation when I was teaching. Validation/invalidation can build up or tear down your self esteem. **A validator motivates and uplifts your natural you.** Think of you as a piece of clay. Michelangelo, an artist, could look at a piece of clay and bring out the most beautiful work of art from what he perceived was inside that clay. You do that when you validate your loved ones.

An invalidator leaves a negative impression on your natural you. In my situation, I was the clay. My new boss perceived my relationship with the schools as a threat to her success. She chose to use negative ways to gain control instead of building on my relationships to help her succeed. Her main focus in this situation was to gain control by tearing apart my work of art.

I was so glad I had taken that class and knew about invalidation. I had learned an invalidator (I like to call them knee gators) is someone who cuts you off at the knees so you don't feel like you can stand on your own. A knee gator is also someone who tries to take away a very valuable aspect of your personality—your own choice.

Chronic invalidators could easily be compared to the black holes in space—they suck the "matter" out of everything and everyone around them.

Remember Maslow's theory of the five basic human needs? Does invalidation (leaving negative impressions) affect your love and belonging needs? From my experience, it sure did. **Negation most certainly affects esteem (feeling valued) and self fulfillment needs.**

What does invalidation (negation) look like? It would be a person who *continually*:

Makes you feel uncertain/ inadequate (you don't know what you're talking about);

Blames you for everything (it's your fault we lost that account, you didn't meet with them enough);

Points out your flaws and uses words like always/never (you never remember to bring homework home or you always forget to take your pills);

Asks you why you can't do something right (I know how to tweet, why can't you get it);

Corrects a story you are telling (Oh, that fish wasn't that big);

Uses humor to bring you down (You're stupid, oh, I'm just kidding);

Interrupts you after asking you a question (starts talking to someone else in the middle of your answer).

Invalidation doesn't happen with just words. Negative body language, eye rolling, and manipulative physical contact (putting pressure on your shoulder or the back of your neck) are signs of someone trying to control instead of guide you. Compliments are rarely given, if at all, from chronic invalidators.

Obviously, most people do not invalidate on purpose—it seems to be a learned habit. A child who is loved **unconditionally** is willing to listen, willing to be wrong, and willing to look at why he or she chose a behavior. **A child loved, but with a steady diet of negative validation, can start to feel controlled, inadequate and angry.**

It is a natural byproduct for an invalidated child to start defining his or her self as bad or wrong and begin to act out. What are the chances this child could inherit and pass on a cycle of negativity—feeling inadequate, angry, controlling, and unwilling to listen, be wrong, or honestly look at why they did something?

What if that child is the adult you—and you continually invalidate yourself?

How to Stop a Cycle of Invalidation

First, remember that you were given the gift of choice!
Second, learn to identify invalidation and **choose** not to allow it.
Third, quit making excuses for someone, including you, who invalidates.
Fourth, feed yourself and any invalidator a steady diet of lovable, capable, and responsible!
Fifth, set boundaries that build HONOR AND RESPECT.
Sixth, divert invalidation or defuse it. How? Choose to speak up. "When I hear you constantly correcting me, etc., it bothers me. **Please stop**." When you catch yourself doing it to yourself, tell yourself to STOP. (And cancel, cancel, cancel!) You could choose to change the subject through humor. "Why in the world would you or I say that?"
How else could you avoid those pesky knee gators?
Seventh, you could choose not to be around them. I recently heard someone say, "Sometimes, people do not **deserve** my attention." OUCH!
When you remember Jesus Christ only got 11 out of 12, you realize some people are just not on the same page at the same time as you.

One of the brightest kids I ever taught was a natural knee gator because he always had to be right. While everyone wanted to work with him on a graded group project (he helped them get a good grade), no one wanted to play with him on the playground. (He was annoying and spoiling the fun of playing a game.) One day he came in early from recess and was visibly very upset.

He'd been ousted from every game he tried to play because he argued with everyone on the tiniest of details. He certainly wasn't on the same page at the same time with his classmates on the playground!

That day this child came in early from recess. He started working at his desk while I worked at mine. All of a sudden, he jumped up and said, "Mrs. Hinkly, I know who I want to be! I want to be Scott Foresman—he wrote the math book and he wrote the science book—that's who I want to be like because he knows everything."

I was pretty stunned, but must have had a wry grin on my face. Watching my reaction, he looked puzzled. I told him Scott Foresman was not a man, but a publishing company—it was a combination of many people writing those books.

He said, "Oh, I can't be him?" I told him that the good news was he could become a writer and actually write books—he certainly was extremely capable.

He seemed to calm down about being right after that—he didn't have to be the really smart kid who knew everything. The pressure was off and he found a new vision for his future. It was not as important for him to correct others; it became more important for him to focus on his own choices. He found his natural personality.

That child caught on fast! Sometimes, with child invalidators, it takes time to get your point across. One of my brothers was a knee gator. The trouble-maker brother chose to get attention from our parents by picking on my sister and me. However, he crossed the line when he physically harmed my sister. My dad stepped in and my brother ended up cleaning the chicken coop for a month. Even though he still teased us now and then, he never physically harmed us again.

When you feel invalidated by adults who are supposed to love and support you, your vision of who you are and what you are capable of achieving can vanish. However, history has taught us those negative impressions have caused some better tomorrows. How?

A great example of <u>learning</u> from invalidation is the founding fathers of the United States of America, who wrote our Bill of Rights! Many of them came from families that left their beloved home countries and led a revolution to create a new country (separate from their old one) because they had been invalidated or persecuted for their beliefs. Our better days are because of their experience and wisdom.

The founding fathers provided safe boundaries and expectations for us to grow and prosper in a democracy. **A Bill of Rights sets boundaries that model honor and respect.** I was in a team of four teachers with 100 students for both fifth and sixth grade. We set the stage for writing a Bill of Rights for our team by sharing our expectations of ourselves. We had a responsibility to **teach** the required curriculum using auditory, visual, and kinesthetic methods so everyone could learn; **provide** a safe, pleasant environment where everyone was valued and equal; and **encourage** growth by making learning interesting and rewarding.

This is the sixth grade Bills Of Rights that was written by our students after we taught U.S. government. I think our students learned well from those original founding fathers.

- I have a right to be safe. This means I will be treated with kindness. I can walk and be careful of others. I will treat others as I would like to be treated. I will stand up for others when they are in danger of physical harm and they will do the same for me.
- I have the right to be educated. This means I can express myself without being interrupted. I can listen, I can pay attention, and I can get my homework done. **I can appreciate the opportunity to learn.**
- I have the right to know my property is safe. This means people will borrow only with my permission, replace it if they break it, put things away, and return found items.
- I have the right to be respected. This means I can listen and I can be heard. I can look at the speaker and others will look at me when I speak. I can stand up for myself and others will support me. I can make good decisions.
- I have the right to be happy. This means I will be included and accepted by all. I have my own feelings. I will be treated as a friend with trust, loyalty, and I will be supported by my peers.

- I have the right to be at peace. This means people will let me work quietly. I will be treated with consideration and dignity. People will encourage me, keep promises, and honor my requests of secrecy.
- I have the right to accept proper consequences for my mistakes. My peers and I will abide by the school rules and state and federal laws and will be punished if we choose not to.

We discussed what proper consequences meant and agreed that it would be helpful to remind each other before reaching the point of needing a consequence. For example, if someone started talking during a test, a person nearby could remind them by pointing to the Bill of Rights posted in the room.

When a Right was broken, we discussed it in a matter-of-fact way, without yelling or blaming. We asked, "What expectation did you lose sight of; what will you do to keep it from happening again?" We used the Bill of Rights for many years. Nine times out of ten, it worked. **However, it doesn't work if someone thinks he or she is above the law. It also doesn't work if it is not consistently enforced.**

Truthfully, a Bill of Rights for a country, classroom, or family is no different than the rules and regulations used for a football or basketball game. While each person on a sports team is valuable, each person is part of a team (group) that works together to achieve a goal. It's comforting (and important) to know what you can or can't do during the game. A Bill, like rules/regulations, exists to promote a level playing field for everyone. Everyone can succeed!

A child in a classroom with agreed-upon Rights knows the boundaries. Success thrives with this kind of groundwork. When the children walked in our rooms each day, they had a clear idea of the expectations. It took away the fear of getting into trouble for no apparent reason. It erased the guilt when a mistake was made because they were treated with as much respect after a mistake as before. It cleared away unnecessary worry. They honored each person's right to learn and achieve goals.

I also found if I made a mistake that affected them, it was critical for me to apologize. It helped to point out what I could have done differently. For instance, one day I didn't pay attention to the time and we were late for lunch. I apologized and asked for their help. One child volunteered to remind me, if I needed it, a minute or two before lunch.

I found my students to be **more responsible and accountable** when I used the Bill of Rights. A Bill of Rights is a tremendous technique for setting boundaries and modeling respect. With a classroom bill, everyone (not just the teacher) can take ownership of classroom management. It works in homes, too! Your family can write a Bill of Rights using this same process. The key is to ask them how they would like to be treated first.

Did you notice the positive wording of the Bill? **There are no DON'TS.** When I was young, my youngest (still older) brother had a habit of drawing an imaginary line between us and would tell me, "Don't cross this line." He would tell me not to, and I always would. He would hit me; I would tell on him. I processed the word "don't" as an invitation to **do.** We both got what we wanted from our parents—I got a hug, he got sent to his room away from his pesky sister.

When I became a swim teacher at 12 years old, I discovered that "don't" was a word that just didn't work with any little kids. If I said don't run, they would keep running; if I said walk, then they would walk. I learned to say what I wanted instead of half of what I didn't want.

What do you want? When I was younger, I wanted to be a cheerleader. I didn't get it my junior year in high school. I asked that youngest brother why. I had practiced and was good at it. He laughed and said, "The cheerleader voting is a popularity contest; everyone in the school votes. If you want to be a cheerleader your senior year, keep practicing AND be genuinely nice and kind to everyone."

How did he go from hitting me to giving such wise advice? I did exactly what he said, and I became a cheerleader. My brother taught me how to BE. **Because I learned to honor and respect people, it changed my whole life.** I initially started being genuinely nice and kind to attain a goal—become a cheerleader. However, it became a habit that made me feel good about myself.

He gave me a key that naturally opened doors for me. Because of my first husband's work, I had to apply to teach in three different school districts in three years. There were hundreds of applicants; I was hired each time. Besides having a teaching certificate and being prepared, I also had a habit of being nice and kind. As one principal put it, "I hire teachers with good personalities, like you. They are usually my best teachers."

When this brother died, several people cried on my shoulder. They all said, "He was like a brother to me!" I was thinking, *"How do you think I feel—he IS my brother."* I decided to smile, listen to the stories, and be genuinely nice and kind. He had a PhD in Educational Administration and was a master of guiding his family and colleagues toward better tomorrows. He certainly guided me in the right direction. **Everyone mattered to my brother; he was genuinely nice and kind to all. Why choose any other way of being?**

Lessons on how to Validate Your Self and Your Child

My parents used a farm mentality to validate my siblings and me. Okay, what does that mean? It felt like sometimes our city farm seemed to matter more to our parents than me. Not true! We were taught about life's ebbs and flows by stories of animals, nature, etc. Why? It can be confusing for young children to know they matter. If a parent has to work a lot or move away from home and can't be there for them, does this mean that parent doesn't love them? As a child starts school, he or she might see other kids with toys or money or things and start to compare what they own to what someone else has. Do these 'things' have anything to do with showing your loved ones they matter or are valued? We had to be 'schooled'!

> *My grandfather (a farmer) had to have his children help during planting and harvesting season. My dad learned and grew to understand the natural order of their life as farmers. A generation later when my dad had to travel for work, I didn't get to be with him. I began to wonder if I mattered to Dad because he was gone so much.*

What is the moral of this story? Things are not always as they seem.

We sometimes forget to teach our children about the whole picture. My dad was gone so he could make money to put food on our table. He had valued us first, and we had no clue. That is a hard concept for a child and my parent's had to **explain** this concept to me. I'm glad I learned it because I had to explain to my daughter why I, as a single parent, had to have two jobs that took time away from her. Once we talked, she was so relieved; she hadn't done anything wrong. It was what I had to do for us to survive and she understood. When she turned 15 years old, she got a job to help me help us.

The first lesson my parents taught me was to focus on the "moral" of people's stories!

For example: *A friend of mine was a farmer's wife. When her pigs had a litter and there was a runt, the female pig (sow) would usually reject the baby runt. My friend had to feed the runts with syringes of pig formula, which was a huge time commitment. It took a lot of time away from her children and she was desperate for a solution.*

On this farm, they had a sow named Bella, who had lost her whole litter several years earlier. Bella had become depressed and psychotic—for years she tried to commit suicide by running in front of the tractor. Seriously! Bella finally succeeded in getting hurt and was put in the barn. Guess what? The runts found Bella and she was miraculously able to feed them. My friend's problem was magically solved!

When pork prices began to drop, they sold all their pigs but one—Bella! She lived with the cows until she figured out how to bypass the electric feeder and the cows got sick from eating too much. Bella was separated from the not-as-smart cows and she got fed slop from family dinners. Heaven! Bella fulfilled her purpose by feeding the runt children and my friend honored Bella by giving her a sweet retirement instead of making her into a ham.

If a pig knows its purpose, birds migrate to the same place every year, and salmon swim upstream to spawn, then there must be a <u>natural awareness and order to life on Earth</u>. The indigenous plains tribes intuitively followed this natural rhythmic instinct of the buffalo (their food/shelter/clothing source) so the tribe could prosper.

What is the moral of this story? Trust the natural rhythm of life: Not getting your way one day (like Bella) can blossom into a chance for something even better tomorrow!

The second lesson my parents taught me was: plant seeds today for tomorrow's harvest.

In the 30 years I was teaching, I would ask my students if they knew what they wanted to do when they graduated. As the years passed, more students had a difficult time coming up with an answer. My theory is that they had problems knowing what to say because some of the careers they ended up in were not yet invented. Learning all they could was like planting seeds.

My students had to handle the unexpected turns of their yesterdays that created their generation's new career opportunities. You are your own student and teacher for a reason. As we age, we have to adapt to ever-developing paradigms. What you always did is **not** what you will always do! I planted the seeds: I used to teach computer skills. Today's harvest: I ask for my grandchildren's help. (They take to technology like a fish takes to water.) They can help me adapt and adjust to the progress of today's inventions.

The third lesson was to use my experience (and others') as a self growing tool.

After my work invalidation incident, I (like Bella) was depressed. What helped me get over my own woes? I thought about my experience with one of my former students who was the epitome of picking herself up from unexpected events. *This child had a mother who had died of a drug overdose and her dad was in prison and wanted nothing to do with her. She was living with her grandmother, who had just had a heart attack.*

I was her sixth grade teacher. She didn't complete homework, she didn't listen, she was preoccupied, and she was late—to name a few of the behaviors I noticed. Yet she was smart and had the capacity to learn well. After several discussions with her, I finally uncovered her biggest fear—she thought her grandma was going to die. She felt alone and definitely felt God was not helping her.

I remembered experiencing this fear with my own daughter. She was scared to death something would happen to me, her only living parent. She insisted I have a will naming her uncle as a guardian, so she could quit worrying. Keeping this in mind, the first thing I did was to contact my student's grandma and suggest she name a guardian for her granddaughter.

This child also needed to feel successful, so I set a homework time for her at school. She and I talked and came up with some positive affirmation cards for her: I love myself; I am capable of choosing actions and emotions that help me succeed; I am responsible for completing my homework and my home jobs. She was to read them and say them six times a day.

Indeed, her grandmother died two years later; she was adopted by her minister's family. She stopped by to see me several years later and the transformation she had made within herself was incredible. She was happy! She had graduated from high school and was going to a community college. Her adopted family treasured her and her new mom told me she was a wonderful model for their own birth children.

Remembering her journey helped me get over myself. No matter how hard life can get, I always have choices. **What I think, do, and say is my choice.** When I choose to focus on the best in me instead of reacting to "what seems to be" at the time, I can move forward with grace. You and I can choose to walk softer in our own shoes.

I was taught I matter enough to guide my thoughts for more positive outcomes.

Walking softer within my thoughts has made unexpected things happen! When I got over my woes of losing a job, I decided to alter my thought to *"something better will come along."* I met a woman at a casino; we talked and became friends. One day she asked me if I wanted a job. She just happened to be the event manager and I was hired to help her put on parties and tournaments. I got paid to talk to people! How appropriate was that?

I was taught to be mindful of how valuable my words and actions are (especially for children).

I picked my granddaughter up from day care and was trying to drive across a busy street. As my frustration rose, I finally said out loud, "I don't think I can get across this street."My three-year-old granddaughter quietly replied, "You can do it, Grandma."

Oops, what was I saying? Her words helped me calm down and cross the street. Children pick up on our words and actions. I tell her she can a lot and obviously she's hearing it from others. **Believing you can achieve a goal is the first step in making it happen.** I believe what goes around comes around. **You will get back from your children your own words and deeds.**

I was taught to understand the bigger picture. . .

If Earth is THE BIG SCHOOL, why wouldn't life be a series of lessons to help me become my best Self? Eventually, some child in this world will need me to do my part to help him or her grow—either directly or indirectly.

I was taught you don't have to see the Sun to feel its warmth.

A star like our Sun has a burning desire to make our days brighter. In fact, even on the darkest of days, the Sun still shines. You are the **STAR** in your life and your children's life. You are as important to them as the Sun; even in the darkest of times, you can still encourage your children to shine.

I was taught to think about how I want to be remembered when I pass on.

To paraphrase a wise nun, it may be a long time coming, but you can kind of expect it!

No one dies when you are remembered by those who matter to you. You choose by your thoughts, words, and deeds HOW you will be remembered.

"Humankind has not woven the web of life.

We are but one thread within it.

Whatever we do to the web, we do to ourselves.

All things are bound together.

All things connect."

Chief Seattle

CHAPTER 4

The Fourth Key for Better Tomorrows: Trust What Lies Within You

"What lies behind us and what lies before us are tiny matters compared to what lies within us." **Oliver Wendell Holmes**

I once had a student who was a master of continually demonstrating the power of what lies within us. At 11 years old, she was the most natural empathetic child I have ever met. **The thing is, she was totally unaware of her unique and exceptional innate talent.**

This child was so gifted at reading people and situations; she could walk in the classroom, look at someone, and quickly say something or write a note that lifted that person's troubles. She also loved to read her stories in language class—and by doing so, she somehow brilliantly modeled the language concepts I was teaching at the time. Like most children, she had no idea that these particular skills were beyond the "norm".

My theory is we are born with a treasure chest full of talents and gifts that help us reach our purpose or reason for being. That child had the ability to naturally read people and situations and it is a gift she could choose whether or not to further develop. You are no different than that child. You were born with an abundance of natural resources and preferences. **Ignorance of your talents limits your character development**. So, why not educate yourself?

Psychiatrist Carl Jung believed:

> **"Everyone is born predisposed to certain personality preferences;"** and
> **"Human behavior is predictable and classifiable."**

Dr. Jung felt people experienced self preferences, or uses of their own predisposed traits, when using their minds or focusing their attention on something. He looked at how people naturally tended to take in information, process it, and make decisions. For example, would you prefer to run an idea by others or digest that idea on your own? **Your preferences are considered part of your personality type, and they contribute to HOW you develop your character.**

The Myers & Briggs personality test is a result of Dr. Jung's theory. It is given to determine your psychological preferred traits. The test determines where you put your attention and get your energy: Extroversion or Introversion? **Extroversion** means you get your energy by being actively involved (**external**), while **Introversion** means you get your energy from your inner world—ideas, memories, etc. (**internal**)

The next two traits are about what you tend to pay attention to—information that comes from your outer **Senses** (what you see, hear, touch, taste, and smell); or information from impressions, patterns, or inner **Thoughts** (analysis and intuition).

The third pair of the Myers & Briggs test describes how you like to make decisions. Do you prefer **Thinking** (you like to analyze, be consistent, and logical) or do you prefer to rely on **Feelings** (points of view, values, what is best for people involved)?

The last two pairs describe how you like to live your life. Do you tend to be **Judging** (you prefer a more structured and decided lifestyle) or **Perceiving** (you prefer a more flexible and adaptable lifestyle)?

I learned so much about myself when I took the Myers & Briggs personality test online on their website. There are many tests available that determine preferences; in fact, many businesses are now using Productive Index Tests to ensure employee's natural traits are being used well. **You don't have to take a test to find your <u>basic</u> natural talents and preferences.**

Think back to your childhood inclinations and preferences! From my experience with my grandchildren, their natural preferences were noticeable early on. At five months old, one granddaughter reached for building toys (like blocks) and loved purses—to keep her small toys in one spot. She naturally prefers to create an organized structured environment. Another grandchild couldn't get enough of writing. At one year old, she would use her sister's crayons and pencils to write anywhere she could. (No surface in the house escaped her handiwork.) She literally would leave her mark wherever she went. My oldest granddaughter loved to run when she was young; now she's a member of her high school's state champion soccer team. Thinking back to my childhood, my favorite toy was a child-sized teacher's desk. Learning and teaching are natural inclinations for me. These are some examples of noticing a person's predisposed traits or self preferences. They are classifiable and fall into categories that can give you clues to your sense of ease and life purpose.

Did you notice the Myers & Briggs test focuses on where you get your energy? **Like everything in nature, you have your own innate energy.** The Sun produces its energy through burning hydrogen and helium. You produce energy by eating and breathing. Every body in our solar system has an energy field. Your own electromagnetic energy field even has names; it is called *chi, ki, prana,* etc. by Eastern cultures. Western cultures refer to it as the aura or biofield energy.

> I find it interesting that many healers mirror descriptions we use for parts of the Earth to name sections of the body. The Earth has longitudes and latitudes, vortices, and hemispheres; healers use terms like hemispheres, meridians, and chakras—which are energy vortices—for the human body. Our bodies mirror the Earth to the point that some believe our bodies are mini-Earths.

Look at all the resources the Earth has naturally. You have as many resources available to you. Your inner resources may not be gold, but they are just as valuable. Your gold mine is your abundance of inner **Self resources**. (I keep capitalizing Self because your Self is important!)

What have we learned about the Self? We know for sure that the word "self" is a noun (a person, place, thing, or idea). Your Self can be the way people see you act according to the roles you play. However, a complete personality is when your Self exhibits a sense of ease with life. Synonyms for the word "Self" are personality, nature, character, and identity. You are born with inclinations, or Self traits, and feel most comfortable using those harmonizing innate talents.

An example of innate traits or preferences could be the traits associated with a natural leader. Leaders tend to be responsible, focused, goal oriented, etc. It could also be a more defined quality like naturally optimistic. You can **consciously choose** the positive side of a trait, like being responsible, or the negative side, which is being controlling.

The student who was naturally empathetic was a natural healer. She also had a knack for leading others toward new ways of thinking. Do you tend to have the skills of a leader, a teacher, or a healer?

Like everything else in nature, these three broad categories (teach, lead, and heal) have many branches. Trees are trees, but an oak has a different purpose than a pine tree or a fruit tree. Humans are humans, but your reason for being can be as different—like the trees.

Some people are like mighty oaks, some bear fruit, some are pines. The possibilities are endless.

Guess what? From my experience, your Self preferences or innate traits are huge clues to your reason for being (purpose for living) on this Earth. For starters, do you PREFER to:

> **Focus on your Self OR do you like to serve others?**
> **Do you like to express the joys of life OR do you prefer to bring peace to others?**
> **Are you interested in having material possessions, fame, and/or rewards OR are you a personal satisfaction and quiet self-attainment (achiever) type?**

Do you want to build something on your own OR do you prefer to manage and direct others? Do you learn best from life experiences OR do you prefer analytically studying to understand why things are the way they are? Do you want to leave your mark in a positive way on this Earth?

You can learn more about your Self preferences.

1. *Ask yourself good questions.* How do I tend to want to spend my time each day? What sources do I usually draw from for information or inspiration? Who or what seems to influence my decisions? When do I most feel a sense of ease (natural) with my Self and my lifestyle? Why?

2. *Notice how you naturally prefer to learn something.* Do you prefer to see something in writing in order to really understand it? You are a *visual learner*. You would tend to use phrases like "I **see** what you're saying" or "I've got my eyes on that". If you tend to use phrases like "I **hear** you" and do better listening to someone or something—like a book on a CD—you are an *audio learner*. If you have to do it to learn it, you are a *kinesthetic learner*. This would be a person who uses a phrase like "It **feels** right to me". A kinesthetic learner is a hands-on learner.

What does the preferred learning style have to do with someone's life purpose? A career or job that requires a person to sit at a desk all day would eventually become uncomfortable for a kinesthetic learner. A person who learns best visually can feel ill at ease in a job that requires "hands on" tasks all day long such as factory work. Obviously, the audio learner would naturally be better in a job that requires a lot of listening. Our preferred learning style can naturally lead us to careers that suit our personality.

Because civilizations have evolved, humans have the luxury of becoming more specialized—you don't have to do it all in order to survive. People with developed preferences can build better tomorrows. Consequently, I used several strategies at the start of the school year to decide how I needed to teach for each of my students to develop their skills.

The first strategy I used to determine a child's learning preference was to ask a recall question. "What did you have for supper yesterday?" or "What is Grandma's maiden name?" It has to be a question he or she knows the answer to, but has to think about. Watch the child's eyes as he or she thinks of the answer. A visual learner's eyes will tend to look up, an audio learner will generally look to one side, and a kinesthetic learner will most likely look down.

Another way to find a child's preferred way of learning is to pay attention to what he or she notices. My visual grandchild doesn't miss a thing. She reads road signs and notices a thing like a ladder by a house that wasn't there the day before. Another grandchild has to feel or touch everything; she is a kinesthetic learner. My audio learner grandchild remembers and repeats my exact words—often days later—even though she is just three years old!

A key to a child's education and success is to expand opportunities to not only honor a preferred learning style, but to give the child opportunities to strengthen (be at ease) with other learning styles. By the time a child graduates, he or she should be able to make a living using all of the learning styles—giving a child more choice.

Think of what you could do to improve your interactions with a child when you know the preferred learning style. If a child is a visual learner and is asked out loud to do several tasks at a time, more than likely, the visual learner will do one task well and have trouble remembering the rest. It **doesn't** mean the child can't follow directions. If you write the tasks down and give him or her list, the visual child would be able to complete the list well. If you gave the audio child a written list, the child won't know what to do with the list—verbally asking this child is best. It would be unfair to judge an audio learner for struggling with a worksheet with only visual directions. The kinesthetic child needs action words in directions: **walk** down to office and **carry** the papers they give you back. Hands-on learners tend to get into trouble for not sitting still or doodling while you're talking, yet it is how they learn best.

As adults, it is important to know about preferred learning styles—for yourself and your children. Looking back on your past, you may find that you were judged harshly or labeled as dumb just because you were a kinesthetic learner who doodled in a visual/audio school world.

3. Ask your Self, "How am I naturally smart?" One of the best classes I ever took as a teacher was a class on Howard Gardner's Multiple Intelligences Theory. To me, it felt right to look at every child as having some kind of intelligence. Remember the child who felt dumb because he was in reading recovery? It was the Multiple Intelligence Theory that gave me the idea to tell him he was athletically smart. Just as any child likes to be thought of as lovable, any child also likes to be thought of as capable!

If you think you are smart, you are capable of putting more effort in to any task you are given. Thinking you can't follow directions is a recipe for you to NOT follow directions. Thinking you ARE smart and capable is a recipe for success.

Are you smart in language, math, music, or athletics? What if your intelligence is analyzing patterns, interacting with others, or knowing your Self? My theory is every person can develop a skill when he or she feels smart and capable. After all, you do have natural talents and gifts. It is **your choice** to use your gifts either positively, negatively, or not at all.

I had a "ladder to success" poster in my classroom that sums this idea up. On the poster, it said, "If you think 'I CAN'T', you have NO chance of success." Why? "I can't" reflects perceived ability. "If you think 'I WON'T', you have a 10% chance of success" because "I won't" reflects conscious choice. If you think "I CAN", you increase your success rate by more than 30%.

---

4. Review your last major decision. What skills did you rely on? I felt it was time to get a new car. My must haves: Safety—all wheel drive; Ease—hatch back trunk, heated seats for the cold winters, enough seats to fit my grandchildren; Cost—a monthly cost that fit my budget; and

Trust—I chose a reputable model and dealership. I researched online and called my insurance company and bank. I drove a few and chose the car I felt most comfortable driving. I didn't run my choice by several people and get lots of opinions. I rely on Self instinct and I tend to rely on how something feels since I'm a preferred kinesthetic learner.

It is not always what you do that matters; it is who you choose to be while you are living life.

I tend to see life as a chance to BE more than DO. So how did I learn more about my Self? Besides learning about the Birth Order Theory choices, I was fortunate to learn more about my hidden talents when I read about Pythagoras, who lived from 582--507 BC. Who? Pythagoras was an ancient scientist, philosopher, and the founder of the Science of Numbers.

Pythagoras felt every number (including your birth date) and name (given name at birth) had energy. Obviously, my granddaughter naturally did too—her code was numbers. What if we looked at finding your own pass code in a simplistic way using numbers? On your birth certificate, you are first labeled with a birth date and then a given name; could these be clues to your internal pass code or ways of "being" on Earth?

I grew to believe in a common sense theory about numbers and their relationship with individual goals and group dynamics. If you go back to "In the beginning..." the first person on Earth was Adam. One person would obviously be self focused—like an arrow going in one direction—in order to survive and achieve targeted goals.

The second person on Earth was Eve. The second person would be an arrow going in another direction. The second person would tend to be cooperative or a mediator in order to survive. The second person expands the perspective and encourages growth for both people.

When a third person on earth was added—a triangle was formed. The third person brings joy and develops communication skills to encourage growth. A fourth person in a group makes a square and would most likely bring structure and stability to a group. When you add a fifth person, you now have a higher chance of conflict and change. Consequently, the fifth person would be visionary and teach adaptability.

The sixth person would feel responsible for group leadership, while the seventh would teach the group how to move forward in new directions. The eighth person would want to leave their mark by introducing more complex ideas. The ninth person would have to be knowledgeable and wise, a humanitarian, and a catalyst for group evolution.

Whether you agree with this common sense theory or not, most businesses do assign or develop similar group roles. They have CEOs (leaders), CFOs, mediators, secretaries, research and development teams, and so on. The list goes on depending on the size of the business.

I took a series of classes and was certified in Cooperative Learning Techniques. In a classroom, the cooperative learning techniques were much simpler. We assigned the equivalent of a leader, recorder, and timer (a one, a two, and a three). The roles expanded as the groups grew larger. The goal of cooperative learning was to teach children the responsibilities of each role and to give them an opportunity to be each role. (This also increases a child's awareness of the importance of working together.) The group was graded not only on the end product, but also on the way they successfully cooperated.

I loved cooperative learning because my students learned to be good team members and it was an experience they could use in the future when they would be in the work force. They also could use cooperative learning skills at home. A family is a group where roles change as a child develops. The child will have to assume the role of family leader at some point in life.

Cooperative grouping is similar to farm mentality living. At a very early age, I had responsibilities that contributed to the family's success and my own future success. I babysat nieces and nephews at a fairly young age. I have a friend who milked cows at 10 years old, and another who was paid to be a church organist at age 12. Both contributed time or money to help the family survive. Through experience, we learned how to contribute to our "society".

All children still need to learn **how** to become a **responsible** adult. First comes love, then comes capable, then comes responsible. Most children learn how to communicate needs and wants, and then they learn how to get along with others. To be successful or self actualize—make something real or make something happen—a child does best when he or she learns to responsibly develop his or her unique gifts and talents.

This brings us back to the question—what lies within you—what are *your* natural talents and preferences? Without experiencing a variety of opportunities, it could take you a long time to recognize your gifts. I nearly flunked algebra in high school. In college, I had to take a "how to teach math" class and loved math. Why did it take me so long? I could have been good at math earlier! Don't you wish you had a Self manual that made things easier? Computers come with manuals. Why don't children, why didn't you? When I found "the Science of Numbers in modern numerology", it guided me toward **honoring my innate talents and gifts**.

My husband is one of the most natural learners I have ever met. Since his strokes, he's had to revise his talents and gifts. Fortunately, he is very curious and enjoys learning new things.

Unfortunately, he has lost some common sense when it comes to choice. One skill lost in the revision was computer use; he has totally crashed three computers in three years. The last computer he crashed had the computer's repair manual only on the computer! I had to ask for professional help.

Do you ever feel you need professional help with your child? Fortunately, children are generally naturally curious. Unfortunately, common sense most often has to be modeled or taught. When your child crashes or veers off course, think of him or her as a mini-Earth. After all, volcanic emotions and Earth-shattering revelations are natural occurrences that seem destructive, but can be constructive if you learn from them.

Did you ever read the children's book, *The Little Engine that Could*? The little engine was successful climbing a steep hill because it repeated over and over "I think I can, I think I can, I think I can". Life can be like climbing a steep hill, but everyone has natural Self resources that encourage us to reach the top. When you choose to believe "I think I can", you greatly increase your ability to succeed. Your children have a greater chance of success if **you also think they can** be successful. You not only fill in the negative impressions on your precious work of art, you have not robbed the world of his or her skills.

What lies within you is an energized spirit! Like Michelangelo, you get to uncover your possibilities by using your natural resources—a brilliant menu of inborn talents you can develop. After all, what is the greatest resource on earth? It is not gold or oil or precious gems like diamonds and pearls—**it is children**. You are a child of the stars and the greatest resource on Earth is for you and the Earth's next generation to develop and evolve.

Circle the group of words that seem to describe what lies within you!
(Both the positive and negative traits are listed.)

1. Intelligent, courageous, prideful, independent, inventive, creative, organized, methodical, original, determined, individualistic, opinionated.
Aggressive, stubborn, selfish, egotistical, tactless, demanding, willful.

2. Patient, tolerant, peaceful, quiet, agreeable, considerate, understanding, diplomatic, charming, friendly, efficient, cooperative, forgiving, reliable.
Sly, oversensitive, timid, too flexible, self-conscious, indefinite.

3. Talented, joyful, friendly, passionate, artistic, sociable, enthusiastic, creative, charming, interesting, cheerful, witty, imaginative.
Fickle, scattered, domineering, egotistical, lackadaisical, moody, long-winded.

4. Reliable, conservative, firm, steady, hard working, determined, loyal, practical, patient, logical, proud, faithful, methodical.
Stubborn, unimaginative, contrary, opinionated, plodding, stingy, moralistic.

5. Dramatic, adventurous, exciting, energetic, passionate, intelligent, enthusiastic, free thinking, curious, versatile, inventive, futuristic.
Moody, sharp tongued, impulsive, restless, inconsistent, critical, overextended.

6. Charming, unselfish, sympathetic, persuasive, idealistic, considerate, loyal, loving, thoughtful, reliable, honorable, caring, intelligent.
Vain, self righteous, underhanded, outspoken, extravagant, dominating.

7. Mystical, perfectionist, philosophical, thoughtful, intelligent, analytical, pensive, sympathetic, inventive, intuitive, introspective, artistic. Moody, reserved, unrelenting, independent, elusive, shrewd, suspicious.

8. Powerful, charitable, wise, efficient, spiritual, courageous, perceptive, kind, charming, ambitious, sincere, reliable, understanding. Egotistical, money or power hungry, arrogant, dictatorial, overactive, tense.

9. Inspirational, wise, curious, giving, idealist, compassionate, futuristic, philosophical, peaceful, sincere, talented, sophisticated, searching, psychic. Lonely, impulsive, unconcerned, over-emotional, careless, self-pitying.

We often recognize these traits more easily in other people—a spouse, a parent, a child, a boss, etc. There is a reason fables, fairy tales, folk lore, myths, etc., were the first examples of good and not-so-good human traits. I love the thought that I can be mystical and inventive, but shrewd and elusive seems a bit harsh. I have the capacity to be all of those things. However, **I get to choose** which ones I use most often! **What traits have you been choosing to use?**

CHAPTER 5

The Fifth Key for Better Tomorrows: Raise Your Natural You Awareness

When I started teaching a new unit to my class, I first asked the kids what they knew about the subject. I then asked them what they wanted to learn about the subject and would arrange their answers in a PMI form. What is PMI? Plus, Minus, and Interesting! This helped differentiate my students "known" knowledge. A **Plus** meant the information was correct, important, and a must-know. A **Minus** meant the information was "a point of view" that might be correct. **Interesting** was the "wider perspective" that would be exciting to know.

The purpose of starting a unit this way was to build a connection from what they were smart enough to know so they could add what they would need to know. When I introduced the astronomy unit, I found most of my students knew more about astrology. They could tell you their "sign" and some of the traits associated with it. Most couldn't name the planets (or their order) in our solar system, and they didn't know much about the stars or constellations.

Why? Astrology was actually more available to my students (in newspapers and online). I connected their astrology knowledge to the astrological part of the History of Astronomy. By teaching the history and origin of astrology, I was able to use that as a building block for adding to their knowledge about astronomy.

Why would I bring this up now? I'd like to take you on an interesting journey to help you learn more about your innate talents and preferences. I'm using a building block similar to astrology—the science of numbers (now known as numerology). The science of numbers is a belief in a mystical relationship between numbers and physical objects or living things. The science of numbers also defines common characteristics in people and life themes, and delves into the relationships of one human being to another.

Pythagoras was the father of the science of numbers and is acknowledged for contributing to the development of mathematics. He also influenced philosophers like Plato and Aristotle. I believe several psychologists (like Dr. Jung) did study the history of human behavior, including Pythagoras' theories, before developing their own, more modern-day theories of human behavior.

When a child is born, most people figure out the birth date's astrological sign. I add the birth month, day, and year together to figure out the child's possible talents and gifts. My theory is the birth date number traits are the "mystical" traits the child is most at ease using. Interesting! Try it. Add your birth date—month, day, and year—and reduce it to a single digit. How?

1. Start with the numerical value of your birth month.

January	1	**July**	7
February	2	**August**	8
March	3	**September**	9
April	4	**October (10) or**	1
May	5	**November (11) or**	2
June	6	**December (12) or**	3

2. Then find the numerical value of your birth day.

1, 2, 3, 4, 5, 6, 7, 8, 9, or 10 becomes 1; 11 becomes 2; 12 becomes 3; 13 becomes 4; 14 becomes 5; 15 becomes 6; 16 becomes 7; 17 becomes 8; 18 becomes 9; 19 becomes 1; 20 becomes 2; 21 becomes 3; 22 becomes 4; 23 becomes 5; 24 becomes 6; 25 becomes 7; 26 becomes 8; 27 becomes 9; 28 becomes 1; 29 becomes 2; 30 becomes 3;

31 becomes 4. By now, if you are pattern smart, you have noticed the double digits are added together to get a single digit.

3. Finally, find the numerical value of your year of birth.

1945= 1+9+4+5= 19; 1+9= 10; 1+0 = 1. Write your year, including all four digits of the year, and keep adding them together until you get a single digit. It is much easier for children born after the year 2000. 2+0+0+4= 6; 2+4 = 6!

4. Now add the month, day, and year all together! For an October 13, 1971 birth date, you add 1+1+3+1+9+7+1=23; 2+3=5. (Keep adding until you have a single digit). This talent bank number is 5. For December 3, 2004, you would add 1+2+3+2+0+0+4=12; 1+2= 3. You can shorten the process by first adding the month of December (1+2=3) + the day (3) + the year (2+0+0+4=6), which equals 12; add the 1+2= 3 talent bank.

Whew! What is the single digit of your birth date? It is your own personal energy (talent bank) number. **The beauty of using numbers is you can use it for a baby (who would never be capable of taking a personality test).** Your birth date energy (referred to as birth path or birth force number) is a small slice of the science of numbers. It tells you the energy (possible natural talents and preference strengths) you can draw on during your life journey.

If you're like me, I was originally skeptical of the "numerology" theory, but the science/math teacher in me decided to research it. Why? I couldn't figure out where my grandchildren got some of their natural talents and preferences. They exhibited traits that weren't from mom or dad or anyone else in the family. At six months old, where were some of these obvious natural talents coming from? I found them in their birth energy talent bank number.

My next step was to connect the building blocks of what I already knew. As a certified "hands on" healer and a Yoga student, I studied the chakra system (a Sanskrit word for "spinning wheel"). I had a friend who owned one of the first Aura Cameras. It uses Kirlian photography (color) and biofeedback (using the acupressure points in your hand) to measure the energy of the seven chakra centers in your body. Teaching science, I saw seven visible colors in a rainbow (using prisms). I play the piano. There are seven keys in an octave. What a coincidence!

The more I looked, the more the building blocks kept stacking up. I taught energy (heat, light, and sound) in science; Native American lore (including their animal lore) in social studies; and fairy tales, myths, etc. in reading. I began to wonder—if everything has energy, would animals have a talent bank? How about fairy tales or cultural characters? I am able to physically see trees' energy fields. (They are not all the same.) Why wouldn't everything have its own version of an energetic talent bank?

It was an educational and eye opening journey. I included these natural teachers in my written descriptions of the talent banks (for the three learning styles). *I gave my brother and his wife a description of their energy. His reaction was, "Keep going with this". My sister-in-law politely read hers, then her face literally paled! She gasped, "Why did you choose the color orange for mine. I have done stain glass work for years and always put a piece of orange in the bottom of everything I do—and I didn't know why!"*

My sister-in-law loved it so much she had a 'party' and invited friends over to learn about their birth date talent bank. She also requested the written talent bank description for her granddaughter, who was turning 12. Her granddaughter was having trouble with bullying from others. When she read what I wrote about her she was so excited. She said to my sister-in-law, **"Grandma, this is all about me—this is who I am!"** *She started doing better in school by focusing on her gifts instead of listening to opinions. My sister-in-law, on each grandchild's 12th birthday, makes sure each one gets their energy talent bank description. Her oldest granddaughter is now a senior in high school and wants to be a behavioral psychologist.*

Why did I listen to my brother and sister-in-law's opinions? My brother taught biology, was a guidance counselor, a school psychologist, and ended up with a PhD in Educational Administration. My sister-in-law was a nurse with a Master's degree in geriatric counseling. She hurt her back, so she became a teacher and taught reading and language in a middle school. Their opinions mattered! Furthermore, my oldest brother has a Master's degree and taught chemistry and physics. He also agreed that I should continue with birth energy talent banks.

Since then, I've started a business and have done hundreds of them over the past five years. One day, I was depositing money from an event, and the bank manager asked me what I did. I used her birth date and described her own energy talent bank; her employees wanted to know theirs, so I did a quick read for each of them. The bank manager said, **"I just did productive indexes on my employees and your information is identical to what I found in the tests I gave."** My business ended up as small business of the month, and talent bank descriptions were on display at my bank! How ironic.

Needless to say, I knew the key I stumbled on was an insightful way of raising awareness about inborn traits. As I looked closer at these ancient systems, everything fell into place when I compared the Nine Digits to: our solar system, the chakra system, and our skeletal system. They are an easy way to build an organized foundation of all of nature's unique teachers.

When you look at the Nine Digits like a backbone, the number **one** is at the base of the spine. Interestingly, the base of the spine is called the first chakra center in Yoga. The chakra centers are similar to the Earth's spinning energy centers, like Sedona, Arizona; they are the human body's energy focal points. Each body center (chakra) has a corresponding color and theme. The Nine Digits, in the science of numbers, have the same basic theme.

> The main purpose of the birth energy descriptions (using nature's teachers) is to raise your awareness of the possibilities within you. Whether you agree or not with the birth energy (talent bank) theory, it can expand your vision of you. It is an opportunity to think about your Self from a different perspective.

For me, the relationship between these unique "teachers" and the Nine Digits is remarkable. We can examine the relationship of one number to another and look at common patterns with new vision. Each number has its own personality traits within the "number group" personality traits. Are there some patterns we can find and some generalizations we can make about numbers?

Do two, four, six, and eight have something in common other than being digits and even numbers? Do they have harmonious vibrations or energy? Will we see some common characteristics in odd and even number groupings?

One, three, five, and seven are not only odd numbers, they are also prime numbers. Generally, the people with a birth date or given name that totals up to a one, three, five, or seven have strengths that help them develop the Self first. They tend to process information inwardly and use abstract ideas to draw conclusions. These numbers generally prefer to make decisions based on ideals. **Ones** focus on self development, **Threes** are about creative expression, **Fives** are about being free to learn from experience, and **Sevens** are about learning all you can so you can share. All odd numbers do eventually like to share their creative efforts with others by expressing or modeling an idea, sharing knowledge, or teaching others using their experience.

Two, four, six, and eight are even numbers and a great addition to other numbers. Generally, the people with a birth date or given name that totals a two, four, six, or eight have relationship themes. They tend to process information by discussing it with others, use more practical ideas to draw conclusions, and make decisions based on sound principles. Even numbers tend to have skills that include others first. For instance, **Twos** bring harmony and peace, **Fours** bring structure and stability, **Sixes** bring love and guidance, and **Eights** bring order and a strong will to make a difference. The number nine has the knowledge of all the digits. Even though it is odd, it is not a prime number. However, it is magical! As a Nine matures, he or she tends to grow outward into more humanitarian efforts and ideals.

Did your birth date reduce down to the single digit One? The first visible color in a rainbow is red; the first vibration on a scale is middle C. The first, or root chakra, is the center for identity and survival. The first object in our solar system was the Sun. Connecting the ancient sciences was like putting a puzzle together.

Many fairy tales match the One energy. The story of Aladdin and the Magic Lamp is about being initiating and active by using our clever mind and our natural intuitive magical talents. Several animals also matched the One energy. The fox is clever, creative, flexible, and exhibits strong survival instincts. The fox is also independent, dedicated, and loyal, yet a fox is also seen as a pioneer and a leader—like the main traits of a One.

Does your birth date add up to a One birth energy?

One by itself is independent, self attaining, and a pioneer. Working with others, the One is a natural leader; working alone, One is a pioneer. Red, the Sun, the Fox, Aladdin and the Magic Lamp, all mentioned above, are associated with the number One. Each of these naturally active symbols reinforces the theme of the One. The key words are **Independent, Creative,** and **Self Confident.**

What other words can describe the One talent bank using the PMI theory?

Plus Traits	Minus Traits	Interesting
Determined, Reliable, Positive, Progressive, Leader or Promoter tendencies	Stubborn, Bossy, Egotistical, Lazy, Aggressive or Self-absorbed tendencies	Original ideas, Creative, Clever, Perceptive, Honors courage of convictions

How have I seen these traits in my family? My oldest brother has a One talent bank. As a teacher, he was chosen to grade national Chemistry AP tests. He created jobs for his fellow teachers by hiring them to build houses in the summer. He was honored by Rotary International for his exemplary service and Habitat for Humanity for volunteering on all 130 houses built in Lincoln, Nebraska! He argued with me that he was not a leader; he finally agreed that he does model an ideal of leadership. He is a pioneer and has led others forward in new directions! Like the Sun, he just is; he didn't think his accomplishments were out of the ordinary.

Does your birth date add up to a Two birth energy?

Two is associated with the second chakra—the center for relationships. Consequently, fostering harmonious relationships is the theme for the Two. Orange is the associated color and the note D is the associated sound. Since the reflective Moon (Earth's only natural satellite) is in a harmonious balanced state with Earth, it is a Two teacher.

Other teachers are: the spider, like Charlotte in *Charlotte's Web*, who brings like-minded people together for a purpose; the Fairy Godmother, who magically makes great things happen; and the wise tribal Priestess. Naturally thoughtful, considerate, and flexible, Twos have a natural capacity to listen well and model compromise. Key words are **Harmony, Cooperation,** and **Balance.**

What are some of the Two's possible talent bank PMIs?

Plus Traits	Minus Traits	Interesting
Handles details well, Adaptable, Gentle, Sensitive to others, Diplomatically persuasive	Prefers to <u>not</u> lead, Fearful, Timid, Ignores his/her Self, Unaware of his/her value	Dislikes conflict, Good organizer, Insightful, Sympathetic, courage of convictions Gracious, Peacemaker

In my family, two of my sister-in-laws have the Two talent bank. They kept the family close after our parents died by hosting family gatherings. When I had an emergency, they traveled several hours to be there for me. They listened well to my problems and asked good questions for me to decide my best possible outcome. People tend to gravitate to a Two energy—they generally have a lot of friends and are well respected in their communities. Most Twos, however, dislike being the center of attention!

Both sister-in-laws were and are extremely aware of others needs. One started her church's second-hand store and the other was in charge of her Assistance League's School Bell Program (responsible for giving clothing to children who can't afford them for school).

Does your birth date add up to a Three birth energy?

Three is associated with the third chakra—the center for creative power and self esteem. Consequently, the theme is to express the joy of living. Sunny yellow is their color, and the note E is their sound. Jupiter, known as the greater beneficent planet, helps the Three spread happiness. Other teachers are: the outgoing impish Dolphin; Mother Goose, the original story teller; and the creatively wise, earthy Empress.

Threes are naturally charming, fun-loving, and lovers of life. Innately talented in some form of communication or artistic expression, they bring feelings to the surface. Key words are: **Expressive, Sensitive,** and **Joyful.**

What are the number Three's possible talent banks PMIs?

Plus Traits	Minus Traits	Interesting
Creatively imaginative, Friendly, Charming, Happy, Helpful, Loves to have fun	Scattered, Trivial, Moody, Sensitive, Gossipy, Critical, Too easy going	Talented with words, Artistic, Curious, Inspirational, Intuitive, Optimistic, Powerfully entertaining

In my family, one of my granddaughters has a Three talent bank. She is nine years old and doesn't really have the filters we learn to adopt as adults. Consequently, she has been accused of lying because she answers questions like, "Did you do that?" with very imaginative stories. She rarely has a simple yes or no answer. Adult Threes like to hear people's stories and love to offer solutions to the problems. Threes tend to be very much like their animal, the Dolphin—they like to be socially connected, but free to satisfy their own curiosities of life.

Most Threes have a tendency to show a variety of emotions and naturally express joy well. Consequently, they can be seen as quite dramatic at times. While they worry easily about others or show concern more quickly than most, they can be a huge source of comfort to the people they love.

Does your birth date add up to a Four birth energy?

Four is associated with the heart chakra—the center for love and peace. The Four's theme is to serve others by promoting order and stability within groups. Peaceful Green—the color of nature and renewal—is its color, and the note F is its sound. Like distant Uranus, Fours can "see ahead of their time" and are perceptive.

Other teachers are: the evolutionary Rebel, the powerful visionary Eagle, and the active assertive Emperor. "The Emperor's New Clothes" story teaches the Four to use intuitive discernment to avoid life's pitfalls. Fours are natural managers and have a flare for re-framing ideas and building better tomorrows. Key words are: **Stability, Order,** and **Service**.

What are the number Four's possible talent bank PMIs?

<u>Plus Traits</u>	<u>Minus Traits</u>	<u>Interesting</u>
Responsible, Honest,	Stubborn, Bossy,	Patient, Sincere,
Determined, Practical,	Rigid, Inflexible,	Faithful, Capable,
Likes routine,	Strong likes/dislikes,	Selective, Perceptive,
Organized,	Gets easily frustrated	Inspires Confidence
Conscientious and	over restrictions and	and Achievement
down-to-earth	limitations	through hard work

In my family, another grandchild has a Four talent bank. At seven years old, she manages her space well and everyone else's that seems out of place to her. She is naturally concrete/sequential; she likes schedules and tells you what she wants. She is ready in minutes because she lays everything out the night before a new day. She likes to feel safe and will hide things to protect them from harm. She remembers things well and will correct you if she thinks you're wrong. People, even adults, tend rely on her ability to remember and find lost things.

Most Fours are excellent managers and hard workers who will work tirelessly, sometimes to a fault, to make sure a job is done to their satisfaction. Every detail is important to a Four; if a job is not done well, it is not worth doing; then, a Four won't finish the job.

Does your birth date add up to a Five birth energy?

Five is associated with the throat chakra—the center of well being. The Five's theme is to learn from life experiences and communicate truths to others. The color, Spiritual Blue, encourages freedom of expression and the note G is their sound. Adventurous Mercury, the creative wandering messenger, is a Five teacher.

Other teachers are: the honorable White Crane, who is comfortable in a variety of settings (land, sea, and air); the magical insightful Wizard; and the Hierophant, a bringer of light into the world. Fives are generally bright, charming, and enjoy celebrating life. Changeable and flexible, discipline grounds Five's visionary ideas. Key words are: **Freedom** and **Constructive Awareness.**

What are the number Five's possible talent bank PMIs?

<u>Plus Traits</u>	<u>Minus Traits</u>	<u>Interesting</u>
Enthusiastic, Active,	Restless, Erratic,	Talented, Versatile,
Adaptable, Bold,	Impatient, Nervous,	Amusing, Analytical,
Loves Variety,	Loses interest, Rigid,	Curious and quick
Presents ideas well	Doesn't like routine	thinker, Loves to be
		free to explore

My daughter and several friends have the Five talent bank. Most of them did not enjoy school because they tend to learn best from hands-on experience more than most numbers. They are all quick witted and think outside the box easier than most people. They also don't like to be boxed in—consequently, they prefer to travel and meet a wide variety of people. Fives are very good with people and get along easily with any personality type. They tend to speak their mind and have a big heart for giving to and helping others.

Naturally resourceful, imaginative, and clever, Fives tend to overextend their own resources to make a difference for those around them. They all can tell good stories and are naturally more animated and detailed in their descriptions.

Does your birth date add up to a Six energy?

Six is associated with the Third-Eye chakra—the center of perception and acceptance. The Six's theme is to promote peace, love, and balance in families and groups. The color Indigo is a symbol of knowledge and intuition, and the note A is their sound. Venus, the planet of love and beauty, models stability and harmony.

Other teachers are: the productive Bee, who makes life bloom; the tarot Lover card promoting unity and acceptance; and the responsible Hansel and Gretel, who model resourceful use of creative thoughts and actions. The Six's magnetic personality can bring comfort and wise counsel into their world. Key words are: **Vision, Acceptance, Love,** and **Responsibility**.

What are the number Six's possible talent bank PMIs?

Plus Traits	Minus Traits	Interesting
Appreciative, Kind,	Interfering, Anxious,	Comforting,
Protective, Generous,	Controlling,	Conscientious,
Sympathetic, Friendly,	Worrisome,	Creative, Idealistic,
Wants the best for	Too Selfless,	Good-natured,
loved ones	Opinionated,	Harmonious,
	Sacrifices own	Capable of
	goals, People take	Humanitarian,
	advantage	worthwhile goals

My husband and all of my grandsons have the **Six** talent bank. They are enchanting and charming unless they are not valued by the people they love. They are thoughtful, helpful, and appreciate opportunities to serve others. They have a strong sense of "right" and have little tolerance for what they consider stupid actions. They are curious and appreciate the finer things in life. They are not afraid of hard work and love to have fun with family and friends.

While a **Six** has an attractive magnetic quality about them, it is also easier for a **Six** to take on more responsibility than most of the other numbers. They do not like to let their loved ones down and are hard on themselves if they perceive they are not making a difference. They like to be involved in life and tend to be quick learners.

The next three numbers have qualities that are associated with energy above the spine. Consequently, the themes are more elusive and sometimes harder to see within the individual.

Does your birth date add up to a Seven energy?

Seven is associated with the crown chakra—the center of the higher mind and Self. A Seven's theme is to actively learn, then to teach what they know to others. The mystical color Violet promotes understanding awareness and the note B is their sound. Compassionate Neptune brings faith and spiritual truth.

Other teachers are: the Horse, a symbol of balance and forward movement for civilizations; the Charioteer, who blends strength with determination; and Peter Pan, whose unique realities captivate others. Bright, analytical, and introspective, Sevens encourage conscious awareness for the advancement of mankind. Key words are: **Openness, Trust,** and **Understanding**.

What are the number Seven's possible talent bank PMIs?

Plus Traits	Minus Traits	Interesting
Curious, Logical, Perfectionist, Searcher, Peaceful, Unique, Approaches ideas from different perspectives	Critical, too Introspective, Rebellious, Not Adaptable, Self-Centered, Intolerant, Doesn't easily trust and "hides" emotions	Discriminating, Observant, Intuitive, Good minded, Analytical, Technical, Unique approaches and solutions to problems

I have a **Seven** talent bank, as do some of my friends. Sevens can seem to be in their own little world like Peter Pan; they can dream up crazy ideas and believe that many things are possible. A Seven tends to be curious, innocent, and possibly more self-contained. They are not afraid of hard work, but prefer to find shortcuts to make things easier for others to learn and connect ideas. Generally, Sevens literally want to learn everything they can and will choose a variety of creative ways to share what they have learned with others, especially as they age. As a Seven, I often find myself being a catalyst for people to adopt new ways of thinking.

Does your birth date add up to an Eight energy?

Eight is associated with the transpersonal—a center of higher light and complex ideals. Eights appear to want material satisfaction, power, and rewards; however, their theme is to leave their mark in a more meaningful way on those around them. The complex blend Magenta is their color, while the note high C is their sound. Ringed Saturn, like the Eight, naturally influences others beyond what we know.

Other teachers are: the powerful Lion who is courageously patient; Beauty of "Beauty and the Beast", who learns to look for the beauty within; and the tarot Strength card. Efficient, strong-willed, and passionate about life, Eights wisely refine their vision and assist others

71

as they mature. Key words are: **Abundance**, **Power**, and **Material Freedom**.

What are the number Eight's possible talent bank PMIs?

Plus Traits	Minus Traits	Interesting
Reliable, Dependable, Realistic, Practical, Organized, Capable, Manages people and projects very well	Overambitious, Exacting, Materialistic, Rigid, Impatient, Intolerant, May focus on money or abuse power	Understanding, Energetic, Far-sighted, Magnetic, Philosophical, Generous, Inspirational, hard working and capable of great achievement

One granddaughter, my good friend, and some former bosses have the Eight talent bank. What they have in common is an uncanny way of getting people to work together for a purpose. Most Eights make great managers and are capable of starting their own business. They tend to be very creative, communicative, and people are generally attracted to join in their ventures. Even my three year old granddaughter can focus on tasks and get people involved with what she is doing. They are all tirelessly involved in life and will work hard to take an idea and raise it to new heights for the benefit of all.

Does your birth date add up to a Nine energy?

Nine is associated with an even higher ethereal center and humanitarian ideals. Nines have knowledge of all the numbers, so the Nines' theme as they mature is to selflessly serve others. The color Radiant Gold is linked to high spiritual qualities just as the higher octave notes are the sounds. Self-assertive Mars blesses the Nine with a fiery will and active imagination.

Other teachers are: the Owl who brings silent wisdom, vision, and guidance; Snow White, who inspires living in the moment by letting go of the past; and the Crone, the wise inner teacher. Idealistic, warm, caring, and a natural leader, a Nine's magnetic personality brings tolerance and thoughtful wisdom into the world. Key words are: **Wisdom, Integrity,** and **Humanitarian.**

What are the number Nine's possible talent bank PMIs?

<u>Plus Traits</u>	<u>Minus Traits</u>	<u>Interesting</u>
Sensitive, Philanthropic, Imaginative, Idealistic, Inspirational, Humanistic, Aware of others and wants a better world	Aloof, Unaware, Self-centered, Quiet, Dramatic, Moody, Disenchanted with life's ups and downs	Empathetic, Deeply Caring, Passionate, Wise, Broad-minded, Tolerant, Capable of making great and lasting changes

My youngest older brother had the Nine talent bank energy. He was the one who advised me to be genuinely nice and kind and the one who used to hit me when we were children. He was sometimes disappointed with people's decisions and was somewhat like Snow White in that some people did not always honor who he was. However, he never let anyone change his perspective and made a huge difference to the people around him. He learned to make the most of who he was by cultivating the positive and interesting gifts in his talent bank. Most Nines are comfortable with others and easily adapt to new situations.

Did you notice that **Ones** are active and the opposite of the receptive **Two**? **Threes** are sensitive and the opposite of the practical **Fours.** **Fives** (experience first) and **Sevens** (learn first) are inner growth numbers that eventually share their wisdom, while **Sixes** (promote peace) and **Eights** (promote tolerance) are more outgoing numbers. You could group, as some modern numerologists do, One, Five, and

Seven as numbers that rely on thinking. Three, Six, and Nine are grouped as creative mind numbers, while Two, Four, and Eight are thought of as "taking care of business" numbers. The digits have been grouped together innumerable ways.

If your birth date energy is the number One, is it better than a Two birth date energy? Absolutely not! Every number has value! What is the value of looking at your Self using these ancient sciences? It helps you remember that you have choice and a multitude of possibilities.

What if you don't agree with the talent bank number description in relation to how you see your strengths? You were given a second identity key that you were labeled with when you were born. Maybe the traits associated with your given name at birth are the ones you are relying on more at this point in your life?

Whatever your thoughts, the most **Interesting** aspect of looking at yourself through the science of the numbers is you begin to realize the following:

"The privilege of a lifetime
is being who you are."
Joseph Campbell

CHAPTER 6

The Sixth Key for Better Tomorrows: Be Open to the Coincidences of Your Name Legacy

What's in a name? Ask a new parent! I've seen many a new mother and father agonize over THE name. After all, a name is a legacy they are bestowing on their child. Do you name the baby after a relative, do you choose a "modern" name, or do you pick one that sounds great with your last name? Do you choose a name that begins with the same letter as the firstborn, or do you wait and see if the child looks like a certain name? So many choices!

A legacy is a birthright handed down from the previous generations. This includes your heredity—the transfer of genetically controlled characteristics such as hair and eye color—and some personality traits and talents. However, your genetic material or DNA is still uniquely your own.

As you age in your environment, you develop some preferences and mannerisms from your family. My son-in-law's body type is very similar to his birth mother, but his mannerisms are more akin to the parents who adopted him. Mannerisms are more than gestures—they are unique habits a person consistently exhibits. My step-daughter is a hair twister and my brother was a belly rubber. I'm a belly rubber, too. It was a mannerism I (and my brother) picked up from our dad. It gives me a sense of ease when I'm piecing together concepts.

What's in a name? Some Native American tribes named a child by the first "sign" they saw after the birth—like a Running Deer. Some of the same tribes allowed the child to choose another name at the age of 12 according to the animal that seemed to be the child's greatest teacher. The movie "Dances with Wolves" was actually the tribal name given to Kevin Costner's character in the movie. For the tribe, the name was an identity that described a talent, strength, or possible preference that could help the tribe survive.

Your given name at birth is important. Years after I was born, my mom told me my middle name was her second choice. My cousin (born a few months earlier) was named Lois Marie. My mom was mad; that was the name she wanted. I became Lois Carol. I was going to change my middle name when I got married and my last name changed.

When I discovered Lois Carol meant "song of goodness", I decided to be grateful for the serendipity of my middle name.

Your given name at birth is the first name you were given, whether it was from a biological or an adoptive parent. If you change any part of your given name, for whatever reason, it changes how people perceive who you are. It does not, however, change the legacy of your original birth name. For instance, a numerologist friend thought I had the legacy of the number Six. I don't! She had used my married name instead of my given name at birth.

Your given name is the second identity you are given or were labeled with when you were born. In the science of numbers, the given name at birth energy is called the "destiny" or life purpose number—it is a clue to your reason for being on this Earth.

When I was teaching, another strategy we were taught to use when introducing a new curriculum unit was K-W-L. The K stood for what do you KNOW. The W stood for WHAT would you like to learn. The last one was asked at the end of the unit. The L stood for what did you actually LEARN that was useful?

So, what do you **know** about yourself and **what** would you like to learn about yourself? What can your name legacy teach you that you didn't know before? For me, it wasn't much of a surprise.

However, I learned to not judge myself for my natural preferences or inclinations. For example, I absolutely need time alone to analyze and process information. I had beaten myself up for years because I didn't always want to party when my friends did. I had wondered what was wrong with me. The answer was: nothing. I just need alone time.

I also came to peace with my life journey. How was that possible? I had some situations that helped me be a better teacher because of my experiences. Those experiences, like being told I was not smart enough to go to college, made me a more understanding and compassionate person. I have been able to walk in someone else's shoes to help him or her grow because of my own experiences.

I am a **Seven** birth energy (my talent bank) and a **Seven** given name legacy (my life purpose). My natural talent and name theme both are to learn all I can so that I can share what I know with others. When did I discover this fact? I uncovered this knowledge about my 20th year of teaching. Furthermore, I was born into a family with a father who was an educator and a mother who taught piano lessons.

My four older brothers were teachers and my older sister was a preschool teacher assistant. What a coincidence! I had a family that naturally encouraged me to learn and share. Imagine the coincidences you can uncover!

How could you possibly use numbers for a name? Pythagoras used the natural order of things. If you use the nine digits, you can organize most language alphabets numerically.

1	2	3	4	5	6	7	8	9
A	B	C	D	E	F	G	H	I
J	K	L	M	N	O	P	Q	R
S	T	U	V	W	X	Y	Z	

A, J, and S have a value of 1; B, K, and T have a value of 2; C, L, and U have a value of 3; D, M, and V have a value of 4; E, N, and W have a value of 5; F, O, and X have a value of 6; G, P, and Y have a value of 7; H, Q, and Z have the value of 8; and I and R have a value of 9.

For example:

> If the birth name is: T H O M A S A L V A E D I S O N
> You would add 2+8+6+4+1+1= 22; 1+3+4+1=9;
> 5+4+9+1+6+5=30

Make the 22 from Thomas a 4 (from 2+2=4), use the 9 from Alva, and 30 from Edison becomes 3 (because 3+0=3). So the given name at birth energy of Thomas Alva Edison is 16 and 1+6=7. Thomas Alva Edison invented the light bulb. He certainly used his conscious awareness to en"light"en mankind—the main theme of his number Seven life purpose.

Let's look at another example:

> If the birth name is: H E L E N A D A M S K E L L E R
> You would add 8+5+3+5+5=26; 1+4+1+4+1=11;
> 2+5+3+3+5+9=27

Add the 2 and 6 from Helen and you get 8, the 11 from Adams totals 2 and the 27 from Keller adds up to a 9. So 8+2+9=19; add 1+9= 10 or 1. Helen Keller was a One destiny or life purpose number. Even though Helen Keller appeared to be extremely limited by being both blind and deaf, she earned a college degree and was a respected author, lecturer, and political activist. Her One energy is that of a pioneer and a leader; she made things happen against all odds.

Write your given name at birth, use the number values from above for the letters, and add them all together until you get one digit. You have uncovered your name energy or legacy! You will generally share similarities with your name family, as they teach you how to be or not be. However, it is how you choose to use the character traits that bring you your own unique personal success. According to the science of numbers, your name is a clue to your life purpose.

The One Name Legacy—Leader and Pioneer

You are blessed with innate qualities associated with
your given name theme that inspire you to accomplish
your own life dreams and goals with ease.

You are like the Sun, our only source of radiant light, so it is easier for you than most numbers to ignite your inner passion for outward creative expression. Consequently, you naturally possess a sense of self worth, a powerful imagination, a bright mind, a determined will, and a unique enthusiastic perspective that generates a variety of opportunities for growth. Independent, clever, assertive, adventurous and a pioneer, you like to blaze new trails and encourage others to follow your lead. Improving your world not only energizes your spirit, it fuels your passion for your own personal attainment.

Your spirit soars when you discover innovative ways to make your world a better place by expanding your innate good character, learning to use your creative ideas toward a meaningful purpose, pioneering new ways of finding solutions to problems, and utilizing your natural leadership qualities to model for others how to reach for a higher quality of life.

Sources of inspiration for you are: the color Red, bringing you a passion for life; the Sun, a symbol of creative will and initiating action; the clever Fox, who brings a magical spirit to your efforts; and Aladdin, who teaches you to wish for the best for yourself and those you love.
Key words: Independent, Individualistic, and Self Attaining.

The Two Name Legacy—Peacemaker

You are blessed with innate qualities associated
with your given name theme that inspire you to
create peace and harmony in your world.

You will have a variety of opportunities in your lifetime to bring people together for a common purpose. Consequently, one of your greatest gifts is the ability to easily adapt to a wide range of people and situations. Furthermore, you're blessed with an amiable spirit and outgoing personality that naturally attracts people to you.

Like the Fairy Godmother—you enjoy magically making things better for those around you; in fact, you are seen as a source of comforting strength because of your sensitivity, patience, tolerance, diplomacy, and tact. Because you are broad-minded, loyal to your loved ones, and compassionate toward humankind, you tend to avoid conflict and generally prefer to guide people toward compromise and agreement.

As you mature you learn how to remain calm under pressure and balance wisdom with forethought. You can thoughtfully adapt to outside influences and have the ability to develop wise listening skills. You can foster cooperation and promote peace.

Other sources of inspiration for you are: the creative color Orange, blending passion to promote compassion with joy to cultivate cooperation; the creative reflective Moon, teaching you to accept the natural ebb and flow of life; and the Spider, like Charlotte from *Charlotte's Web*, who teaches you to creatively and artistically weave minds together for a common goal.
Key words: Relationships, Cooperation.

The Three Name Legacy—Communicator

You are blessed with innate qualities associated
with your given name theme that inspire you to
communicate the joys of life to those around you.

You will be given many opportunities to use your entertaining imagination and innovative insights to inspire, motivate, and uplift those around you. Unique, imaginative, bright, and creative, you fascinate and entertain the world around you with your fun-loving and youthful attitude. Expressive and playfully amusing, you enjoy finding delightful ways to encourage new ways of thinking beyond the ordinary.

Your natural talents include good communication skills, a bright and clever mind, a flair for sharing your delightful ideas with others through your words and actions, a charismatic personality, and boundless energy. While you tend to rely on your cleverness and instincts to make your own decisions, it is the excitement of sharing your decisions and life experiences with others that you find rewarding. Your adventurous side creates opportunities for you to expand your horizons—your strong communication skills persuade those around you to look at life with renewed enthusiasm. Like Mother Goose, you have a knack for "civilizing" the world around you. Your charm is your happy, sensitive nature and optimistic enthusiasm for life.

Other sources of inspiration for you are: the color Yellow, which brings you joy; the impish Dolphin, who is socially connected and yet feels free to explore; and the planet Jupiter, blessing you with expansive thinking, wealth, and good luck.

Key words: Creative, Expressive, Joyful

The Four Name Legacy—Organizer

You are blessed with innate qualities associated
with your given name theme that inspire
you to build toward a better future.

You much prefer structure, order, harmony, and peace in your life. Consequently, you tend to be logical, practical, determined, hard working, and down-to-earth. Interestingly, you also have the ability to intuitively know things ahead of your time, enhancing your capacity to plan well for the future.

With natural organizational skills, a great eye for detail, a bright mind, and a rebellious spirit, you easily connect separate ideas in unique unconventional ways. Since you naturally feel responsible for your family, friends, and your community, you do best when you build your own secure and stable home environment first. You build better tomorrows for those around you by relying on your common sense and by balancing work, family, and friends.

Like the fairy tale, the "Emperor's New Clothes", you are a natural ruler and love encouraging growth in others. You also have a mystical childlike awe of life that can make you feel vulnerable when you lead the way for humankind.

Other sources of inspiration for you are: the color Green, which brings peace, balance, and hope; the Eagle, a symbol of power and great vision; the rebel planet Uranus, which teaches you to re-frame old experiences for new meaning and insight; and the cultural character the Emperor, who reminds you to use your creative will power for the good of all.

Key words: Limitation, Order, Service

The Five Name Legacy—Promoter of Freedom and Progress

You are blessed with innate qualities associated
with your given name theme that inspire you
to learn and grow from life experience.

Like adventurous Mercury, you prefer the freedom of traveling your own path on your life journey. Consequently, you are adaptable, adventurous, fun-loving, innovative, intelligent, curious, and fascinating. You enjoy generating a wide variety of opportunities in all areas of your life to broaden your insight so you can understand why things are the way they are. For you, using the knowledge you gain from experience is the way you affect change for the betterment of mankind. When you expand your vision for your own personal growth, your enthusiasm bubbles over to others lighting the way for those around you to expand their vision. Your charismatic personality, along with your zest for investigating the unusual, is enchanting.

While your heart believes in magic and mystery, your logical side demands rational answers that can cause you to question what others would not. Like the wizard, you know how to take an idea, analyze it, make a decision, and quickly bring it into reality. Consequently, you are very observant, independent, fair-minded, and progressive. You are blessed to have an unusual flair for celebrating your love of life.

Other sources of inspiration for you are: the White Crane, who awakens intuition and spiritual justice within you; the color Blue, a symbol of creative expression so you can share your experiences; and the Wizard, who teaches you to use your charming personality to celebrate life's magic.

Key words for your greatest development are: Constructive use of Freedom.

The Six Name Legacy—Enthusiast

You are blessed with innate qualities associated
with your given name theme that inspire you to
enhance the lives of those around you.

Your natural preference is to promote growth in yourself and others
through service to those around you. Consequently, you are blessed with
a charismatic personality, a generous spirit, strong leadership skills, high
ideals, and a heightened awareness of righteousness and responsibility.
You much prefer to lead, even if it's by example, and you work well in
a structured setting with set rules.

Intelligent, wise, honest, sensitive, understanding, and devoted to
your family, you do your best work when you feel safe and secure
in your own environment. You enjoy being valued and appreciate
opportunities to support, comfort, and give advice to your loved ones
and those in need. Even though you much prefer to enhance the lives of
others, staying true to your own dreams actually enhances your ability
to serve others. You can blend a practical business mind with your
heartfelt ideals to encourage success and your greatest strength is your
ability to think and act with wisdom and forethought. You can inspire
others to appreciate the beauty that can be found in everyday life.

Other sources of inspiration for you are: the planet Venus, bringing
you love and harmony; the Bee, who teaches you that many lives
would not bloom without you; the color Indigo, blessing you with
knowledge and enchantment; and Hansel and Gretel, who teach you
to be creatively resourceful.

Key words: Responsibility, Love, Balance

The Seven Legacy—Educator

You are blessed with innate qualities associated with your
given name theme that inspire you to learn and grow
so you can share what you've learned with others.

You are an innately deep thinker and enjoy connecting unique concepts in unusual ways. You also prefer to use your knowledge and blend it with your own expansive perception to communicate your vision for evolution to others. Consequently, you enjoy using your sharp mind to analyze people and situations, ask good questions, and delve into what you don't understand. Studious, observant, independent, imaginative, charming, and friendly, you enjoy people from all walks of life, which raise your awareness of the ways of the world.

Ingenious, introspective, thoughtful, peaceful, and affectionate, you have a calming magnetic quality that causes others to look toward you for direction. Consequently, you will be blessed with many opportunities to raise your awareness. Give yourself quiet time to integrate your thoughts and exercise your strong intuition; you can refine your ideas and then find a unique way to share them with others.

Other sources of inspiration for you are: the Horse, a symbol of freedom, power, and potential; the spiritual color Violet, which gives you dignity and determination; the planet Neptune, a symbol for independent thought and action; and the adventurous Peter Pan, who reminds you to honor the child within you and creatively soar toward new heights.

Key words are: Analysis, Understanding

The Eight Legacy—Achiever

You are blessed with innate qualities associated with your given
name theme that inspire you to leave your mark on Earth.

You appreciate the satisfaction that comes from being of value to
the people around you. Consequently, you may initially long for power,
success, recognition, or material rewards. As you mature, you learn to
expand your vision of how to leave your mark on Earth in a deeper,
more satisfying way. By widening your perspective and relying more
on your inner wisdom and judgment, you enlarge your tremendous
inherent potential.

Energetic, determined, resourceful, intelligent, and down-to-earth,
your strength is your ability to patiently interact well with others, so you
can positively influence those around you. Your organizational skills
and willingness to work hard lead you to a variety of opportunities for
success. Your sheer strength of character and managerial skills, along
with your ability to accurately assess people and situations, are great
assets.

You innately see beyond appearances to find the true beauty
and value of all life. You understand and appreciate the freedom that
comes from being in control of your own resources. Use your wisdom,
initiative, and cooperative spirit to uphold higher ideals and promote
greater prosperity for all.

Other sources of inspiration for you are: the color Magenta,
bringing you power tempered by thought and calm; "Beauty and the
Beast", teaching you to develop your inner awareness; the planet Saturn,
broadening your perspective and perception; and the Lion, which gives
you courage, strength, and creative will.

Key words: Satisfaction for Self and Others

The Nine Legacy—Humanitarian

You are blessed with innate qualities associated with
your given name theme that inspire you to selflessly
serve others to make your world a better place.

Friendly, caring, sensitive, thoughtful, colorful, flexible, and generous, you model acceptance and tolerance toward all mankind. In fact, you have a tendency to be respectful of all living things. As you mature, you learn to use your sympathetic heart and charitable nature for all life to serve others. Consequently, you have innate talents that will develop as you grow in your awareness of the world: higher principles and ideals, broader perspectives, honorable intentions, visionary ideals, and a gracious spirit. Flexible yet strong, knowledgeable yet wise, your charm is your youthful attitude and pure and innocent character. Because you can encourage evolutionary progress, you will experience dramatic opportunities for your own growth.

Having the knowledge of all the numbers, you have an open mind for new ideas. Not only do you create innovative opportunities for yourself, you can initiate change effortlessly. Your inherent gift for understanding why things are the way they are teaches others to look at the wondrous beauty of life with new vision.

Other sources of inspiration for you are: the color Gold, a symbol for feelings of warmth and a sign of success; the Owl, who teaches you to trust your instincts and vision; the planet Mars, reminding you to be your own person while sharing with others; and the humble Snow White, who knows remarkable wishes do come true.

Key words: Humanitarian, Selflessness, Love

> **Oliver Wendell Holmes once said, "One's mind once stretched by a new idea, never regains its original dimension."**

How did I combine what I already knew about my Self with the **talent bank** and **name legacy** information and come up with a renewed vision for better tomorrows for my Self? My journey began because of my experience with children. Let's see...30 years, 180 days per year, 8 hours per day, multiplied by 30--100 children a year... I had no choice! I had to stretch my mind for them, which in turn helped me grow even more when I retired and had more choice.

It's always good to have a few examples though! What if a person has a **Five** talent bank and a **Four** name legacy like my child does? The **Five** theme is to learn from life experiences, so freedom of choice has always been important to her. In a career, she will tend to be organized and a good manager (the **Four** name legacy). The **Five** talent bank gives her a natural thirst for variety because she tends to learn best from her experiences. Her **Four** name legacy prefers stability in a career. People tend to see her as amiable, capable, and cooperative and she can get along with a wide variety of people. From my experience, her amicability will disappear if you try to control or limit her **Four/Five** combination. (Don't box her in.)

While she has stayed with her main career for the last 12 years, she has had a part time job for almost 25 years. She prefers stability in her work life. Her love of variety is fulfilled by three things: her four children (one is a stepson); her Aura Camera, which allows her to meet an array of diverse people; and her volunteering. She loves to use her experiences to make her world a better place for her children and build better tomorrows for her community.

Since she has a double **Seven** mother who learns from experience and loves to share and a father who was a **One** name legacy (leader and a pioneer) and a **Three** talent bank (an insightful communicator), it is not surprising. Her grandparents had compatible numbers; they gave her a variety of experiences and a solid foundation for her to grow.

My daughter's oldest daughter has a **Three** talent bank (like her dad) and her second daughter has a **Four** talent bank (like her name). What's happening? The daughter with the **Three** talent bank (receptive, sensitive Empress energy) is teaching her younger sister how to be more compassionate while the **Four** daughter (the assertive practical Emperor energy) is teaching her older sister to stand up for herself. My daughter understands and encourages this.

How does it help their family dynamics to realize all of this? As you know, the strongest of us can slip into dysfunctional behavior when events negatively affect us. Think of notes on a scale. A **Three** talent bank is like an E on a piano and a **Four** talent bank is like an F on a piano. How well will they blend in a negative situation? If the **Three's** E becomes sharp with the **Four**, the **Four's** F will go flat! They end up on the same "negative" note, which can affect everyone else in the family negatively. However, in normal situations, they can help each develop a greater sense of ease within their Selves AND learn to honor each others' innate preferences.

To further apply all of this information, let's look at a classroom full of children. I found out as much as I could about my students by asking myself questions. What was their preferred learning style? What were their social and emotional intelligences? Were issues keeping them in survival mode? What innate talents were untapped? What could I do to get the best results for them to learn and grow? Could one child model his or her strength to improve another's weaknesses? I maximized my own students' talents for greater results.

The same is true for any social group. Maximize the gifts of those around you by learning from other people's innate talents and legacies. What can one person learn from another to increase his or her intelligence? How do friends expand your awareness?

You can apply the same principles in a work environment. One purpose of learning about each number is to learn how to get along with a wider variety of people. If I were in charge of a big project, I would choose a **Two** as a facilitator, a **Four** to collect and manage the data, a **Seven** to analyze the data, an **Eight** to refine the details, and a **Three** to prepare the final presentation. If I were having a problem with an employee, I'd certainly review what I know about that employee's preferences before I decided on my course of action.

You don't have to go up to a person you are just getting to know and say, "Hey, when is your birthday and what is your given name at birth?" You can pick up on a person's basic talents and legacies by doing the following.

> **Asking a question**. If someone gives you a one word answer, more than likely that person tends to take in information or make decisions on their own (an odd number). If the person asks you a question in return, you know the person likes to interact with others (an even number).

> **Observation.** I took a class and one assignment was to watch people at a mall. It was an eye opener. One lady had a list and was checking it off, which told me she was organized and made good use of her time. (I would bet she was either a Four or an Eight.) Another couple started to argue and I could see their facial expressions and body language. One was naturally passive while the other was very assertive.

> **Pay attention to the information a person shares with you.** My step-daughter works for a corporation that gives Personality Inventories (PI). Her manager asked her recently about her PI in my presence. They had recently moved her to another position in the company that is much better suited to her talents and preferences. She showed me her PI. Comparing the scores of her company test to her birth date talent bank and her given name legacy at birth, they are identical in identifying key personality traits. How is that possible? Psychology is the ancient sciences' child.

At the beginning of this chapter (on your name legacy) I introduced the K-W-L method we used to introduce new learning. The L is asked at the end of the learning process. At the time, did you wonder if you were going to learn something excitingly useful! *Did you start thinking about. . . not being happy with your job. Did you think, maybe I'll learn if I'd be better off being a health care professional or a teacher or a manager, etc.!"* After all, the name legacy is basically about your destiny or life purpose.

A "destiny" (according to the science of numbers) is not about **Who** you are, it is more about what you **Must Do** in your lifetime. As a **Seven**, I could choose to be any of the above occupations and then share that knowledge with others. **The main theme of a Seven is to learn and share.** I was born into a family that enhanced that theme: learn and share. When I worked at a casino after I retired from teaching, guess what happened? I was placed in a position where I learned my job and then was, more often than not, teaching others how to do the same job well. Either directly or indirectly, I unknowingly have learned and shared all my life—starting with my first job at age 12 (I was a swim teacher). I didn't consciously choose to learn and share. I just felt more a sense of ease within my Self when I was placed in positions to learn and share. You might want to go back and look at the given name theme for your number. Think of the people around you that reinforce or model your theme either in a positive or negative way.

What did you learn about your Self when reading the name legacy descriptions?

When I asked myself that question, I thought of my experience; I realized that I, personally, don't do well learning from someone showing me how NOT to be. Therefore, I wrote my descriptions from how I learn best—from having my highest quality character traits or my most successful ways of BEING as the main focus.

When I began sharing the legacy descriptions with hundreds of people, I found everyone else loved hearing about the best qualities in themselves, too. I've never heard someone say, "I wish I was meaner or dumber or completely self-centered with no friends."

It's kind of like *The Little Engine That Could.* Why would I choose to think negative thoughts when I want positive results? I'm just not going to get where I want to be as fast when I use my assets in a negative way. It is the same for the children you touch. Why would you model for your children how NOT to be instead of a how TO be? Wouldn't it take longer for them to be able to self-actualize or feel fulfilled by who they are if you choose the negative? Which felt better for you?

Did you learn anything about the people who raised you or the children you are raising?

Thinking back to my troublemaker brother, I learned that with my sister and me, he chose to think the word NOT in front of many of his wonderful qualities. He was NOT thoughtful and he was NOT a gracious spirit. He let his birth order supersede his good qualities—choosing to get attention by doing the opposite of what he was capable of. He eventually grew out of those negative choices, but it did harm his relationship with us until we were much older.

If birth order can affect how a person chooses to use their name legacy, couldn't invalidation, feeling we don't matter, or wondering if we're loved or capable or responsible also affect our choices?

From my experience with using the name legacies, it is extremely important to realize every single person on Earth has a choice. Each of us can choose to think the best of our Self, and more importantly, think the best of our children.

My parents used to say, "We've got the best kids in the world!" Do you know how good that felt? Let me tell you how their way of thinking about their six children helped us grow! I moved the furthest away, yet I was told on three different occasions (I was living in 2 different states) that my family was one of the most humanitarian families they had ever met.

It certainly wasn't me they were talking about. I didn't live where these individuals did. I have received numerous compliments about every single sibling. All six of us were teachers. Between us, we taught a total of more than 150 years. Do you know how many kids we touched?

I was helping a friend move and all of a sudden he stopped working, looked at me, and said, "You have changed the world!"

I thought, "Helping you move is changing the world?"

He said, "No, I'm serious! You have taught kids from all over the world and I can tell you were a good teacher. You have changed the world in a good way by teaching all those children." Jim Rinehimer

Needless to say, no one had ever told me that! When I repeated his statement to my retired teacher friends, they were as speechless as I had been. I wish you could have seen the huge smiles on their faces and in their eyes. I know my siblings would have smiled, too.

Whether you agree with the given name legacy descriptions is not the point; what is important? **It is an idea that does matter**. It matters to the children each and every one of you touches to learn as much as you can about their innate preferences, talents, and gifts. Whether you are a parent, a teacher, or a leader, you have an opportunity to change the world one child at a time—just by the way you choose to be with the children in your life. Why would you choose to look at children any other way than to realize that you get to bring out the best in them and love them enough to help them grow?

**Why would you choose to look at your
Self without realizing . . .**

**"It is never too late
to be what you might
have been.**

George Elliot

CHAPTER 7

The Seventh Key for Better Tomorrows: Remember to Turn! Turn! Turn!

"There is a season and a time for every purpose under Heaven."
Ecclesiastes 3:17

Everything seems to have a beginning and an end. Everything is born, lives, and dies (or evolves into something we don't yet have the capacity to know or understand). Everything has seasons; the springs, summers, falls, and winters that are used to describe the cycles of lifetimes. We have seasons of Ages. Civilizations have experienced the Stone Age, the Medieval Age and the Space age. What do seasons or stages have to do with anything? Everything!

While I have a talent bank and a name legacy, there were times when I was simply not capable of using some of my innate skills well. Looking back, I really wasn't ready for a few things I wished for at the time. For instance, it was a good thing I didn't have a baby when I first wanted one. It wasn't time!

Regardless of the Age we are in, a baby still grows into a child that must be given opportunities to learn how to grow into an adult, which also happens in stages! Everything in nature, like the caterpillar evolving into a butterfly, has seasons or stages. Would you put a three-year-old child in the driver's seat of your car to get where you want to go? Not only is a three year old not mentally capable, but physically it would be difficult for him or her to reach the gas pedal or the brakes!

This is why our schools have a curriculum that is designed to be age appropriate. In other words, in each of the subject areas, children will be taught what is appropriate for their brains to handle and retain at their age. At about the age of a sixth grader (adolescence), research our guidance counselor shared with us (as well as my own experience teaching 4th, 5th and 6th graders) has shown that children's brains are actually growing to the point where they can understand abstract concepts better than younger children.

On top of that, you simply can't teach every math or reading or physical education concept there is in one year! That is why schools refer to vertical and horizontal curricula.

Horizontal is what is appropriate to be taught to a child of a certain age (like what a normal third or seventh or eleventh grader can comprehend). Vertical is what the school district must provide for each child in a curriculum area (like language or math) that builds upon last year's skills. That is why schools are referred to as elementary, middle, high school, followed by higher (college) education.

From my own experience, my fourth graders weren't capable of learning much about complex story mapping, yet my sixth graders were capable of learning about and using story maps very well. The main purpose of our schools is to teach the child everything they need to survive and grow in a 13 year cycle—kindergarten through 12th grade—in all subject areas.

We have curriculum areas in a school setting, but I don't know many people who stop learning after high school. What if we, as human adults, can continue to grow with time into a purpose that is more appropriate for this new age of technology? We could take technology classes and leadership, mediation, communication, management, etc., classes that improve our life in the Big Earth School until we graduate to a whole new level on Earth! What would that look like? After all, we have seasons for a reason. We all have times when we are capable of learning what we couldn't comprehend before. What if humans have a nine-year (there are 9 digits) cycle that repeats over and over again at a higher level until we have all the experience, knowledge, and wisdom to evolve or graduate to an even higher level of learning school?

Civilizations evolve. My country—the United States of America—became a country on July 4, 1776. In case you were wondering, if you add the birth date of this country, it is a **Five** talent bank! Hmmm. How appropriate! The **Five** is about the having the freedom to achieve progress by learning from life experiences. If you do the numbers for the name, The United States of America adds up and reduces to the **Nine** energy—the humanitarian number.

If you use the Gregorian calendar like most western civilizations, in any given year you can **add the current year with your birth month and day** to find what grade/season/stage you are in now. The United States, in the year 2015, is in a **One** year. How did I reach that conclusion? I added the 7 (July is the **7th** month) and the day (4) to the current year, 2015 (2+0+1+5=8). So, 7+4+8 = 19 and 1+9= 10 = 1. The United States of America is in a **One** personal growth year. The country is 239 years old in 2015 and has continued to help us learn and grow from the experience of being a citizen of this country.

Isn't that what civilizations and people do? Learn and grow from their mistakes and their greater achievements.

I decided to think that I am continually in school. I could sit back and relax—after all, I've had 30 successful years of teaching children. I did my part. However, it goes against my nature of wanting to learn and share to NOT continue learning and sharing. I think that's why most schools teach children of all ages to strive to be lifelong learners. Maybe that's also why some retirees do so much traveling—to learn from new experiences. How many of you have made the proverbial "bucket list" (a dream to-do list) that you can hardly wait to start checking off? It makes sense to me that we would have opportunities to explore different options as we age. It may be a long time coming, but wouldn't you like to expect it?

For the last seven years, a good friend of mine has asked me each year, on his birthday, for his personal year information. He just turned 80 and looks forward to what he could possibly experience in his new year. So I add it up for him (his birth day + his birth month + the current year), then I give him a copy of his new personal year description.

When I first studied the science of numbers, I learned about the personal year information out of curiosity. To tell you the truth, I wrote them for fun and gave them to a friend (and her mom and dad) because they were curious, too! This 80-year-old man is my good friend's father. He can be skeptical, yet he found that it really described the journey he and his wife were on during that year. In fact, when his wife passed away a year ago, he pulled out her last personal year and pointed out to me why she "graduated" to a higher school that particular year. I was pretty stunned, but his reasoning made sense. She had valiantly fought off her uterine cancer for many years, and during that time, they had both grown with wisdom way beyond their ages. I know he was comforted by this one piece of information—the personal years. It made me realize that each person's journey is unique and one of a kind, just as we are all unique and one of a kind.

However, we all still have being human in common. We all have a purpose and it makes sense to me that we will each continue to learn our entire life, whether we like it or not. Some will learn more than others because of a willingness to expand their capacity for growth beyond their current capabilities. I think we learn to accept the fact there is a time to reap and a time to sow!

While this concept comes originally from Ecclesiastes 3:17, Pete Seeger is credited with writing the song "Turn! Turn! Turn!"

What is my point? Reading this book has put you on a learning curve. You are becoming a **seasoned** parent, teacher, or leader. So, what's next on the agenda?

**Add your birth month, day and current year
(2015) together to get your personal year.**

The One Personal Year

You are beginning a **One** personal year, a special year because Ones are synonymous with new beginnings. For you, this new year starts a fresh nine-year cycle of life. Like a child walking into a classroom for the first time, you may not realize the enormity of the opportunities coming your way. Just imagine what you can achieve knowing what you know now!

What you know now is that new experiences and fresh challenges are a part of life. You can purposely develop your character and expand your horizons. How do you choose who to become now that you know more, or what do you now have time to do? What would you like to achieve next? First, reflect on your heart's desires and achievable options. Then, use your decision making skills and good judgment to take action. Let go of past disappointments and sail toward a bright new dawn. After all, you are the captain of your own ship.

The planetary body associated with the number One is the **Sun**, known as the source of all life on Earth and our power to be. As the only star in our solar system, it is independent and free in its magnificence. Like the Sun, you are one of a kind and have your own purpose. You can be powerfully original. You also get to learn that while it is important to be a star, everyone else will also get to be one, too! Why not shine your light on them where they are now?

The personal animal for the number One is the **Fox**, who knows anything is possible with positive action. The Fox teaches you to quietly develop your plans for success through ingenuity, wise will, and courage. By consciously putting your best foot forward, you will find yourself on an amazing magical journey.

You have reached a stage where, like **Aladdin**, your time has come to wish for what you want. The power of the lamp is in choosing right thoughts, words, and actions for manifesting ideas. You will get what you wish for, so be careful for what you wish.

Red, the color related to One, represents passion and desire. It is a power color that promotes creativity and confidence.

Let your own imagination and brilliance light your way this **One** personal year.

The Two Personal Year

You are beginning a **two** personal year, which is a year of extremes! It is a good news and bad news year; the bad news is you must have patience. The good news is you can consciously develop plans, using a step by step process, to build a stronger foundation for your future. You get to learn to work smarter instead of harder.

The key words for the year are balance and cooperation. Twos are known for their mediation and peacekeeping skills, so remember to not take things too seriously and keep your sense of humor. You may find yourself forming new partnerships and expanding your circle of friends, for this year you can excel within a group using your powers of persuasion, tact, and diplomacy.

The planetary body associated with the number Two is the **Moon**. Just as it affects Earth's tides, it affects us! You only have to gaze at the Moon to realize the varied emotions it evokes. Its strength lies in its ability to so effortlessly adjust and adapt to the forces around it. As a constant reflection of the Sun's light and an inspiration during our dark nights, do you think the Moon worries about its own phases? They are an integral part of its charm. Maybe it's time for you to honor your own stages.

The personal animal for the number Two is the **Spider**. Spiders are accomplished weavers and magical creatures. They are masters of using creativity, exercising assertiveness, and relying on rhythm and patience to reap rewards. Spiders teach you to trust what you feel and to look beneath the surface before diving in to a project.

The Two year is the year of the **Fairy Godmother**. She waves her benevolent wand your way, giving you wisdom and faith. She is a symbol of childlike magic and miracles, constantly reminding you to keep believing. What you think you do not know or can't have, you can know and have. Whatever you think you cannot express, be assured that you can. The color of a Two year is **Orange**. The power of orange comes from its parts—red and yellow. Red brings passion and yellow brings joy.

Dare to reflect, dream, and build for a brighter tomorrow in your **Two** personal year.

The Three Personal Year

You are beginning a **Three** personal year, known as a joyful optimistic year packed with flashes of inspiration for self improvement. You may suddenly discover new ways of thinking, allowing you to develop ideas beyond what you thought possible. What can be imagined can be created! It is also a time for socializing, celebrating, and joyously living. Why not relish life in all ways?

It is a great year for you to express yourself with creativity and sensitivity. You may find yourself inspiring others through your happy-go-lucky attitude, wise words, and caring actions. You may start a new job, travel, take classes, or do other things that help you reach your full potential.

The planet associated with the number Three is **Jupiter**. Jupiter is known as a benevolent planet because it brings with it blessings and luck. As the largest planet in our solar system, it teaches you to expand upon your ideas while upholding the ideals of freedom and truth. With Jupiter as your guide, you can find a new sense of identity and meaning within your own circle of loved ones or even expand your circle of friends.

The **Dolphin** is your animal for the Three year. Dolphins, with their impish smiles and expressive eyes, promise new growth and fulfillment. The animated dolphin teaches you to cheerfully travel through the waters of life to find what you want and need.

Like **Mother Goose** in the fairy tale realm, Threes are masters of written and oral communication. Therefore share your aspirations with whimsy and flair for you have the ability this year to constructively and dynamically create with vision.

The color of the number Three is **Yellow**. A potent color linked to logic and intellect, it colors your world this year with happiness and joy. Feel the freedom to be who you are and take delight in the awesome wonders of life.

Choose to express your Self with joy and creativity in your **Three** personal year.

The Four Personal Year

You are beginning a **Four** personal year, signifying a time to settle in and hunker down to more practical matters. While it sounds mundane, imagine what it would be like to have the power to transform your future. You do have the power this year. Analyze, clarify, and refine your ideas using a step by step process and you will achieve the seemingly impossible.

It takes a strong stable foundation to generate superior outcomes. Consequently, becoming more goal-oriented while relying on a strong work ethic will assist you in manifesting quality results. Powerful creative building tools for this year are your intellect and a new innate ability to understand things using your common sense coupled with new insights that seem to appear out of nowhere.

The planet associated with the number Four is **Uranus**. Uranus, outside the orbit of the seven classical planets, represents mental programming. It marks changes in the way you think, causing you to re-frame your experiences and adjust your own program for mature decision-making. You gain a larger perspective of what is possible.

Your personal year animal is the **Eagle**, a sign of vision, power, and healing. Eagles are associated with the Native American Great Spirit and represent authority, nobility, and mysticism. This raptor understands that vision alone does not create success. You must act upon what you know will bring you satisfaction and success.

As you focus on your Four year, do not lose touch with reality like the emperor in the **"Emperor's New Clothes"**. It is your childlike trust and awe of life that will help you see through folly. Interestingly, the feminine influence is also a key to success in a **Four** year. The Empress represents wisdom, and the Emperor applies wisdom to create a better world.

The Four personal year color is **Green**, a stabilizing hue signifying peace, harmony, and hope. It is the primary color of nature, which balances and inspires you. It is nature in its bountiful plenty that reveals what a divine mind can create with new insight.

Choose ways to build a better foundation for your future in a **Four** personal year.

The Five Personal Year

You are beginning a **Five** personal year, signaling a time of change that will alter your life forever. Imagine leaving behind the monotonous labors and restless life of the past and shifting your present and future to a more joyous and fulfilling existence. It can happen!

The Five year is known for adventure, exploration, and fun. It also represents conflict and change. Just as there was change and conflict within yourself when you moved from elementary school to middle school, you will also experience new opportunities for growth in areas of your life that you may wish to change now. Whether it is your career, home life, or personal relationships, you have the ability to transform them for your greater good in a Five year—a year that thrives on the freedom to choose a variety of experiences.

Mercury, the planet associated with the number Five, is the planet of travel and communication. Because of its short, speedy journey, it is known as the connection maker. Consequently, during a **Five** year, new insights and ideas seem to magically appear from a variety of places. Mercury retrogrades (looks like it's moving backwards) more than other planets, so review your past experiences and choose to change your perspective.

The **White Crane**, your personal year animal, does well in a variety of environments— land, sea, and air. It teaches you to use this ability to adapt to new situations for greater results. Let your creativity soar with focus, wider vision, and renewed effort—nothing is impossible!

Like the mythical **Wizards**, you have the wisdom it takes to master your own life. Freedom, discipline, truth, and honor open new doors for you in a Five year. The Wizard reminds you to work your magic on yourself first. Your success motivates others to reach for the stars.

The color **Blue** is associated with a Five year. Blue is a calming, peaceful color, known to promote communication and self-expression. It inspires you to look up, move forward, and have faith in the divine order of life.

Choose to widen your vision for better tomorrows by trying something new you haven't done before in your **Five** personal year.

The Six Personal Year

You are beginning a **Six** personal year, a time when home is where your heart yearns to be. Your year will be filled with opportunities to slow down and take pleasure in your family and friends. The **Six**, known as a nurturing number, brings you the ability to promote growth through vision and acceptance.

Consequently, it is a year to expand your understanding, wisdom, and capacity for leadership and responsibility. Coming from love, you can give support, wise counsel, and comfort, making the lives of those around you richer. Rely on the divine force of love itself to transport your mind and giving spirit to creatively stimulate and inspire within your community.

Venus, the planet associated with the Six, symbolizes love, harmony, and sharing. This beautiful planet models for us adaptability and flexibility in relationships, encouraging you to trust your instincts. It is a time to come to terms with your past, stay in the present, and develop a kinder legacy for the future.

Just like the fairy tale of **Hansel and Gretel**, who made it through the dark nights lost in the forest, you, too, are blessed with creative resourcefulness this year. These two not only saved themselves, they were able to find their way home to safety and help their loved ones.

The **Bee**, your personal year animal, is a symbol of productiveness. Without the Bee, many flowers and fruits would not blossom. The Bee selflessly serves the greater good of the community and teaches you the power of working together in harmony. The Bee also reminds you to keep your goals in sight and avoid spreading yourself too thin. Just be the best that you can be at each moment in time.

Indigo, the color of the number Six, is a result of mixing blue and violet. It is the color of magic and mystery as well as pure knowledge.

Things happen when two or more are gathered, so paint with a more thoughtful stroke on the souls of those you love.

The **Six** personal year energy adorns you with a new-found idealistic nature and a natural magnetic presence that attracts opportunities to you for you to create a better world.

The Seven Personal Year

You are beginning a **seven** personal year, known as a time to focus on developing your mind to raise your awareness. As a result, you may find yourself either craving quiet time or longing for travel to search for answers to big questions. By examining the quality of your life and questioning your purpose, you learn to trust the wisdom within you.

This journey within helps you understand yourself in relation to others. It is like removing a veil—new insights suddenly appear right before your very eyes. While others may wonder what's up with you, this quest for knowledge is like finding missing puzzle pieces and you finally get to experience another whole picture of life.

Neptune, the number Seven planet, plays a special role within our solar system. It is known as the group karma planet and teaches you to let go of the old and grow for humanity's highest good. To serve a group with compassion, whether it is by caring for others, speaking out, or generating far out ideas, can mend hearts.

The **Horse** is the personal animal for the number Seven. Horses represent movement and balance. Just as the selfless Horse freed humanity from many limitations to transform civilization, so can you make a difference for yourself within your Seven year. The Horse teaches you to move gracefully forward in new directions to realize your own freedom, power, and potential. You will naturally carry others with you toward greater success for all.

Like the mystical **Peter Pan** soaring to Neverland, you can create more than you ever imagined within your own world. By rekindling the childlike awe and wonder of life's magic, you can fly beyond the mundane expectations of today.

The color of your Seven year is **Violet**. Violet is the color of spirituality and brings feelings of dignity and determination.

Open your eyes to the magic and mysteries of the universe in your **Seven** personal year and envision a better tomorrow.

The Eight Personal Year

You are beginning an **Eight** personal year, the year you reap what you have sown. The past several years you have planned, worked hard, and been patient, and now is the time to accept your rewards. By accepting abundance into your life, your power grows and your Self worth soars. Just imagine what it would be like to allow financial gains, promotions, and recognition into your life!

It is important this year for you to gently guide your thoughts, words, and deeds toward the positive. You can build confidence by being assertive and decisive using good judgment. By consciously managing your emotions, you can remain calm, balanced, and capable of handling any situation with sensitivity.

Saturn, the planet associated with the number Eight, represents wisdom and perspective. It teaches you to look at your past experiences as lessons you can use to refine your own perceptions. Just as Saturn stands out because of its unique rings, you can stand out in a crowd by adapting a new way of being.

The **Lion**, your personal year animal, is a symbol of strength and courage. Interestingly, it avoids confrontation using self-discipline, but defends itself fiercely with determination. The Lion also teaches you to use your creative imagination and purposely develop your intuition for greater rewards.

In the tale of **"The Beauty and the Beast"**, associated with the number Eight, it is the power of gentle love that tames the Beast. This beautiful story teaches you things are not always as they seem, so follow your heart and trust what you feel is true.

The color for the year is **Magenta**, the color of initiative. It represents tranquil thought and proper balance. The beauty of this color is its complexity—it is a mix of many colors. You too can mix it up in your life for greater results.

Appreciate who you are and what you have to offer in your **Eight** personal year. Others will honor you when you honor and value yourself.

The Nine Personal Year

You are beginning a **Nine** personal year, a year when hopes and dreams can come true! It is an important time for you because you are completing a nine-year cycle. You can complete projects, gain recognition for your hard work, and finally initiate changes you have longed to make. Just think of all you've learned about yourself in relation to the world and how that knowledge has helped you mature.

Because you are mastering one phase of your life, you will graduate to a new level at the end of this nine-year cycle. Like any graduating senior, you may feel nervous or uncertain about your future. You may also feel both tense and excited about the imminent upheaval and anticipated opportunities for growth. What will tomorrow bring?

Tomorrow depends on what you learn from today. Have you seen qualities in others you would like to have yourself? What you admire in others can be what they admire about you. You can consciously choose to become a greater person by developing your character.

The planet associated with the number Nine is the powerful, fiery **Mars**. It teaches you to listen to your own inner truths and to express yourself by being the original You. It is not about how other people see you. What is important is what you think about yourself.

Your Nine personal animal, the **Owl**, is known for silent wisdom, vision, and guidance. Use your senses, trust your instincts, and aggressively and quietly pursue your goals. Enjoy the intrigue and fascination the Owl's mystery and magic bring to you.

Like **Snow White**, you are learning wise discrimination on your journey toward personal growth. You know change is coming, so be compassionate, tolerant, and understanding toward yourself and those around you. Strive to live your life on Earth happier ever after!

The Nine color is **Gold**. Gold represents feelings of warmth and love while radiating high spiritual qualities.

Appreciate the preciousness of life and all you get to learn to transform your basic talents and gifts to gold in your Nine personal year.

> ## If you change the way you look at things, the things you look at will change!

What does using a nine-year cycle, personal year theory help you do? It helps you turn directions. How many people do you see continually doing what they have always done? It can feel like driving down a road in a rut you can't seem to get out of. If you can be open to the nine-year cycle theory, your life can change for better tomorrows. After all, Eastern civilizations have used a cycle theory such as the 12-year Chinese Zodiac (year of the horse, year of the dragon, etc.) for ages. Using a cycle theory, you can rise above the past and transform from a caterpillar into a butterfly. You learn to walk softer in your own shoes to be a better parent, teacher, or leader.

How did I become a better teacher? I first had to learn a little about quite a lot to be an elementary teacher. I have a Bachelor of Arts degree in Education. What does that mean? I had to take all the normal subject area classes that most Bachelor of Arts take, and then take "How to Teach" math, reading, language, etc., classes.

Since I am certified to teach kindergarten through eighth grade, I had to specialize (have a minor by taking more classes) in two subject areas. My minors are in social studies and physical education, which means I could be a seventh or eighth grade social studies or phys ed teacher only in those two grades. I could not teach math or reading, etc., at that higher level.

There are many tricks I had to learn in those How to Teach classes that really made me a better teacher. In fact, I learned to love math (finally) and understand the concepts I missed in the regular math classes. To this day, I use the skills the How To teachers taught me with my grandchildren. It is extremely important to know HOW to teach, especially when working with children who are kinesthetic learners. You also have to have many tricks up your sleeve with kids who have not had success in a subject area in previous years. You sometimes have a lot of catching up on skills to teach them in a short amount of time.

My point is that you teach your children and help them with homework without any classes other than what you remember from when you were in school (or from what you learn quickly when you look it up on the internet). Yikes! That can be a recipe for frustration for any parent or child. If your child can't learn the way you teach, maybe you should teach the way they learn?

Did you learn how to adjust your style to theirs in the parenting classes you took? What classes? I don't know of many parenting classes that cover everything you need to know about raising and teaching your own child. We used to provide classes for the parents of our students. The guidance counselor would tell the parents about the normal mental, social, and physical developmental levels of children our students' ages. We would include extra classes at night with information about birth order, invalidation, multiple intelligences, or the things I brought up in the first four chapters of this book. However, that doesn't happen so much anymore because of the time commitment it takes on everyone's part.

What can be the result of a teacher, parent, or leader not being well schooled about how to raise, teach, or lead a child? My friend has said many times, when we were observing children that we met on the street or in a store, "You can tell that kid didn't have good role models for parents" (as we watched him or her make poor decisions).

Do you think "that kid" will parent like his or her parents did? Can that kind of cycle be broken? A child who used to chronically make poor decisions can be a good role model for their children if he or she decides to change. It's leaders, who model the ideal of leadership when coaching or interacting with that kid, who can make a difference for him or her.

My theory is that our life purpose or **what we must do**—if we have children or affect children in any way—**is learn** all we can so we can **adapt** to the needs of those children. I have found I can't parent my grandchildren the same way I did their mother. I've had to change to the way they learn because the world has changed. I can also model a better way for them.

For your better tomorrows, start with the child within you. Is it time for you to love your Self enough to grow so you can model greater ways of being for the children you touch? How?

When I was compiling the talent bank, name legacies, and personal year information, I found a sense of ease and actually more peace of mind for my grandchildren's future (like the one who thought God was not helping her find her pass code) as I thought about and wrote ethical guidelines for my own business.

Who thinks about ethical guidelines? Maybe you think about them while you're working a full day, or when you're doing laundry, cleaning, taking kids to lessons/games, etc.? Maybe you think about it at church or when you're playing a game on your phone?

Let's face it—Earth is a multifaceted place to live with so many more choices today than we had yesterday. There's enough going on to keep us busy and entertained and troubled and on/off tasks and on/off balance—more than we could ever have imagined. What is the point here? I am a better person and model for the children in my life when I take time to stop and **reaffirm what I believe in as a parent, a teacher, and a leader**.

My ethical guidelines are as follows.

> While I am the only one like me on Earth, some people's traits will closely resemble mine; others will not. Consequently, you and I will not always harmonize with everyone around us on this earth. It is okay to *choose* when I want to be around someone I can learn from or avoid someone who is teaching me how not to be. When it seems I have no choice and I have to put up with someone or something, I still have a choice with what I think about it and how I react.

> To label a person "a Seven" is simplifying the value of the lessons. Not all Sevens will exhibit their tendencies the same way. One Seven's analytical ability may be weak, but his or her faith may be stronger. It depends on which trait is practiced more. I can become more adaptable if I focus on practicing some of my other given traits.

It is important for me to remember that one number is not better or smarter than another; one number may have a tendency to rely on intelligence over experience or intuition. Each has its place and is of value. Each person I meet has something to teach me so I can learn to rely on all three.

The purpose of personality tests is to determine what roles I prefer to play at home, at work, or within my community. My roles in the outer world can affect how I see my true Self. Developing my complete personality or sense of ease can enhance my effectiveness with children and increase my personal potential.

The talent/name/personal year descriptions are designed to teach people what they may not know or remind them of what they may have forgotten about their Self. If I use the nine-year-cycle theory (I usually feel the change in cycle years closer to my birthday month—a few months before September—instead of in January), I give myself a chance to change the way I look at life. For me, it gives me permission to move on from hard times and **hope** for better tomorrows.

Sometimes, consistent pressure from families, cultures, countries, or work environments can cause such stress that people may act contrary to their natural Self to fit in. It's time to turn directions! If people can recognize how the pressure of these environments can affect their thoughts of their Self, they can use the power within them to change their Self perception and realize that...

"When you are inspired by some great purpose,
Some extraordinary project,
All your thoughts break their bonds;
Your consciousness expands in every direction,
And you find yourself in a new, great and
wonderful world.
Dormant forces, faculties and talents
become alive,
And you discover yourself to be
a greater person by far,
Than you ever dreamed yourself to be."

Patanjali

CHAPTER 8

The Eighth Key for Better Tomorrows: Educate Yourself Before Choosing Your Next Steps!

My great purpose has been to teach. I've not just taught my child and grandchildren, I have been blessed to teach multitudes of children of all ages. I can't even count how many times I asked myself the question *"what's my next step?"* In fact, I took several classes called "The Next Step". I was hoping to get out of the *"if you don't know what to do, don't do anything"* stage. Oh, some of the choices I made? I used to specialize in extremes; I either analyzed situations almost to the point of non-action or I was impulsive.

In fact, one of my most educational stories about myself comes from my teaching days. *It was a simple request. My blind student asked if he could bring his snake to school. Now, I can't think of a year when a child didn't ask to bring a snake to school for science class. So I told him he could. The next day he brought his snake to school in a special box.*

When it was science time, he asked if he could take the snake out and show everyone. A high school student was helping that day, so my answer was yes. I told him the snake's head was at 10:00 and the tail was at 4:00. I was taught to use the hour positions on a clock to let him know where things were. My student reached in, grabbed the snake, pulled it out, and squeezed it too hard. The snake sprayed poop on the nearest kid (who happened to have a behavior disorder). My blind student's hands got slick from the snake's waste and he dropped the snake.

Pandemonium broke out! I had students screaming and jumping on top of their desks, the BD student yelling that the snaked crapped on him (at least he used the "c" word. It could have been worse), and my snake lover groping around on the floor trying to figure out where his pet snake was. All the while the high school helper just stood there and watched.

What did I do? I lightly stepped on the snake. I then told my student to move toward 12 o'clock and he would find the snake under my foot. I asked the high school student to take the snake-soiled student to the bathroom and clean him up. Needless to say, I didn't even think, 'what's my next step?' I just impulsively reacted. I hate to tell you this, but when he went to put the snake back in its box, he dropped it again! We went through the same process (students screaming, jumping on desks, me lightly stepping on the snake). The third time we got it in.

To get everyone calmed down, I asked my students to take out paper and a pencil and write down what had just happened from their own point of view. I turned it into a lesson on how people's thoughts and emotions can interfere with their observation skills. They were amazed at the variety of dramatic stories their classmates came up with when a snake was involved! It actually turned into a great lesson for everyone, especially me.

Most teachers would consider this a disaster, so how was it possibly educational for me? I learned that reading a variety of educational books—Ernest Holmes's *The Science of Mind*, Daniel Goleman's *Emotional Intelligence*, and *Dancing Wu Lei Masters* (Quantum Physics)—had prepared me to cope with this kind of pandemonium. It also helped that every day; I use a healing modality that focuses on balancing the energetic biofield of my body to help my body stay balanced. I had balanced my classroom that morning, too. It didn't hurt that I was a member of the Iowa Dowser's for a few years. All of these resources helped me think and react outside the box. Would you lightly step on a snake without harming it—on purpose?

The snake episode was a rewarding lesson for me because I realized I had raised my natural awareness enough that I instinctively knew my next step, every step of the way, during a minor crisis. That poor snake was as traumatized as we were. It was trying to find a way to escape by slithering under an adjoining classroom door and it could have visited another classroom full of kids!

As I thought about and processed the 'snake event' at the end of the day, I realized the three things I had researched the most on my awareness journey, the **power of thoughts** and the **effects of our emotions** and **energy** had really helped me grow. I'm not just talking about the natural energy forces on Earth, but also the **personal energy** (power or force) that each of us inherently has. Educating myself about these three things helped me turn toward a better direction in my natural awareness growth.

Because I taught science, the first of these three main topics I stumbled on and pieced together was energy! I could learn to guide my thoughts and emotions, but some days I just couldn't seem to think or was overly emotional for no apparent reason. Just as animals can get agitated when they sense a storm coming, you and I can be affected by seemingly silent energy forces. Recently, a solar storm's magnetic dust affected the wireless towers in some areas and cell phones were out.

Astrologers also warn us about Mercury retrogrades. That little planet can energetically be an imp to Earth! However, the largest force is the one that affects us the most: the **Electromagnetic Force (EMF).**

What is EMF and how does it affect us? (In case you forgot from your science class).

EMF is qi or chi—the energy or natural force that fills the universe. Chi is used to express the **energy state** of something like a living thing; it is produced by our breathing and/or eating. It is any energy demonstrating power and strength such as electricity, magnetism, wind, heat, or light. You and I also qualify as EMFs!

EMFs affect us because Earth has a magnetic field caused by our balanced state in our solar system. I was taught that the ocean's tides are caused by the force of our Sun and Moon. What does it do to us? Like the Earth, our bodies are about 70% liquid (causing **emotional tides** for us). Our Sun is pure radiant energy—we wouldn't exist without it—yet unusual sun activity disturbs radio frequencies and can cause static or challenges to our bodies as well.

What is the result of The Earth's mass, rotation, and revolution around the Sun—we travel about 1.5 million miles per day, causing gravity (about 15 pounds per square inch of pressure on our bodies), our weather (causing winds and storms), and it holds our atmosphere! What does this do to us? Our bodies can sense atmospheric changes. We can get happier or more agitated and edgy during climatic change. **What affects the Earth affects our bodies**.

Since energy is a power or force, **personal energy** is a power or force that every person inherently has. Our personal energy field is always "on" even when it's "off". What are some signs of our personal energy power?

Have you ever had a topical injury? The injured spot can feel hotter or colder than any other part of your body. As a healer, the injured spot will push my hand away or pull my hand to it. This is how I find imbalanced energy on a person's body (temperature/pressure changes).

Have you ever had a person standing so close to you it felt uncomfortable? Did you automatically step back? This is what it feels like when another person's energy is not in harmony with your own energy. Your body will automatically resist that energy.

Have you ever been in a store and had to leave because it felt different to you? Using a dowsing rod or pendulum, dowsers can physically show you how far your body energy radiates. They can also sense chaotic or traumatic energy in a place like a store. Again, the energy was not harmonious to your own, so it threw you off balance.

Have you ever felt drained by another person? A person can unknowingly "take on" another person's energy. My friend was taking care of her ill spouse, who was 11 years older. Continued stress and worry caused exhaustion and she became physically ill and passed away first.

Have you ever experienced a whole room affected by one person? Dr. Effie Chow, an American doctor and a Chinese Qi Gong master, showed me the power of **negative energy** by purposely thinking a bad thought about one person, which in turn changed everyone else in the room to the negative. Everyone felt it, and we saw it when we muscle tested everyone (see muscle testing below). She then thought a great thought about the person, and every person in the room changed back to the positive!

Have you ever met a person and immediately felt judged? In a grocery store, a man was shopping while talking on a cell phone. He was inadvertently blocking the aisle and people were glaring at him, which made him want to stand his ground. He looked similar to one of my nephews, so I smiled, and he smiled back and moved. Because I associated him with a positive "twin", he responded in a positive way.

These are perfect examples that I have personally experienced of how personal energy can affect our interactions and judgment with and toward other people and places.

What is Muscle Testing?

Muscle testing is often referred to as Applied Kinesiology. Our body has in and around it an electrical network like a grid. If this electrical network is imbalanced or not functioning well, or is blocked or diseased, your large muscles will be affected negatively. My chiropractor uses muscle testing to determine if my electrical grid is as it should be for my optimal health. When something is not in balance, he adjusts it and checks it again with muscle testing.

Dr. Chow had us use muscle testing to determine whether her negative thought was good for our bodies or not. In pairs, one would hold an arm straight out in front of him or her, shoulder high, and then ask "Is this thought good for my body?" The other person in the pair pushed gently down on the raised arm. The answer was no for everyone—we couldn't keep our arms up. When it was yes, our arms were able to resist the pressure applied by the other person.

Grandma, I Lost the Pass Code to My Brain!

I have been in awe of the incredible energy available to mankind on this planet. The manipulation of chi is the basis of acupuncture, martial arts, and healing arts. How do you think a person can break a board in half by hand and not be physically hurt? There is a natural force within you, and you can direct this energy with practice.

Sometimes people think stamina is energy—do I have enough energy (stamina) for the day? Actually, your personal energy is your bioelectromagnetic field, or chi. Stamina comes from building up your energy, yet your energy naturally fluctuates from day to day. Why? Each person, place, or thing has a frequency or vibration. I can see my own vibration, my bioelectromagnetic field, or aura through Kirlian photography and biofeedback, and it can change at will quickly. Why? **Vibratory frequencies respond to atmospheres!**

What is important to know about frequency/vibration in relation to our personal energy?

- **Frequency is measured in megahertz**. All solids, liquids, and gasses have a frequency. Roses have a high frequency; the color red, has a lower frequency. Solids, like wood, respond to temperature and pressure changes, and you and I react, too. We have learned to adapt to the variety of frequencies we experience—a child still has to learn how to adapt.
- **Frequency can vary according to conditions**. A young rose's vibration will be different than the same rose fully bloomed because of its age. I certainly react differently as I've aged. Children tend toward drama when new conditions arise. As they get older they learn to adapt more easily.
- **The frequency of thoughts and emotions can be felt**. Have you ever been given a "cold shoulder"? Are you attracted to someone's "warm disposition"? Do you "see red" when you're mad and "feel blue" when you're sad? How well do you think when you are sick? Our thoughts and emotions do change our vibrations, and people around us can feel it, especially children.

- **Frequency subtly affects our actions**. Have you kept your distance when working around someone with a cold? What if the cold is an unstable vibration from static thoughts? I have seen students cover their ears or eyes or quickly move away from "people static" (bad vibes).
- **My thoughts, present attitude, and state of mind affect my vibration/frequency, the way people see me, and how I see myself.** I can alter mine to the positive at will, but only because I've learned how. Children have to be taught how.
- **We can't change the earth's mass, revolution or rotation; it just is what it is on this planet.**

If you observe a group of children for a while, you will see the concept of personal energy (and vibratory frequencies) in action very quickly.

The best way I have used the knowledge about personal energy was in my classroom because I understood the dynamics of daily environments. People are a bunch of charged parts. Everyone is energy, like lightning, which is a bunch of charged particles that meet and clash until they ground. Scientists have been able to direct lightning. If scientists can direct a wild energy like lightning, imagine what you can do with your own energy? The key word here is OWN. While you have the power for your Self, children want their OWN power, too. Clashes!

Power struggles (charged parts clashing) happen when one person thinks he or she can overpower others to get his or her own way. One person may decide he or she is right and try to make everyone else bend to his or her will or one person in a group may make an important decision for everyone without their input. I generally do not clash with other adults unless someone makes decisions for me without my consent. Imagine the frustration a child can feel!

Clashes, like lightning during a rain storm, can clear the air and improve the climate. They can also be an opportunity to learn, grow, and inspire, or they can be the deciding factor for you to change a situation. What is true is that each of us can be affected by the climate of our environment and children are more vulnerable, especially during high-energy times like holidays.

In a classroom, I found that a calm, respectful attitude and an awareness of the pressure a child may be feeling improved the classroom climate. Facial expressions, body language, and how a child interacted with others were all clues I looked for when my students walked into the room. By taking a minute to pay attention to a child with static energy, his or her attitude could be adjusted for greater success. I basically filled their personal energy bucket for a better day.

How do I manage, strengthen, and improve my personal energy to be a better parent, teacher, or leader? By choosing what I feed my body, mind, and soul with my thoughts, words, and deeds.

Thoughts guide our words and deeds (actions), so they are extremely important, especially if you work with children. A friend of mine recently reminded me to keep my thoughts pure about my grandchild, who is a little three year old who has been pushing against her limits lately. What I think is what I will get, so I better turn my thoughts to the positive or we're in trouble. I remembered my favorite quote about the subject of thoughts by Benjamin Disraeli,

> **"Nurture your mind with great thoughts,**
> **For you will never go any higher than you think."**
> **This is the key to working with children;**
> **Nurture their minds to go higher than they now think!**

If you could physically see a child's thought, it would be like a pebble tossed in a pond. If I pick up a pebble (thought) and toss it on the surface of a pond, you will see a ripple. My thoughts are the equivalent to the ripples that appear on the surface of the pond—they are what I do and say. That thought (ripple) circles out and affects everything else in the pond. So do my words and actions. They circle outward and affect everyone around me (including me). It is like a thought creates a series of events.

When the **quantity** of thought overcomes the **quality** of thought, like you will find with most young children, it is harder for them to focus or make choices. Do they have a choice? Most animals will eat the same type of foods and either fight or flee. Humans have a lot more options. I can't imagine what life would be like without the enormous number of choices I have. We teach children to make a choice between two things, and then gradually increase the menu to three (or more choices) so a child can eventually feel a sense of ease with making choices.

When given a choice, I usually end up making a decision; hopefully, it is an informed decision. I was once told that a teacher makes about 10,000 decisions a day. Egads! It is a big responsibility to make decisions for more than myself. The decisions I make often affect the energy or climate of my work environment and most certainly affect my home life climate.

A ripple effect of thought is communication. Every time I communicate a thought—through my body language, speaking, or writing—I produce and transmit my signature energy or vibration. How have I raised the quality of my vibration and improved my thoughts?

Through Reiki, I learned how to raise my personal frequency. It feels like I'm turning a radio dial and tuning in to a new station that is at a higher wavelength. I know this because I had consistent aura pictures taken during this time. You don't have to be a Reiki master (teacher) to consistently raise your energy, thoughts, and emotions. Prayer, meditation, positive affirmations, books, inspirational speakers, etc., can all open your eyes to raise your awareness. **Deciding to change is the beginning of change.** This first and most important step of thinking is the one I can leave out. The second step is to realize that what we think, we create, so we must CAREFULLY CHOOSE what we think. The third step is to understand that humans, of all species, can purposely decide to manage and direct thoughts to enhance lives. How is that possible? If you pay close attention to your body language, words, and deeds, you can see the thoughts behind your words and actions.

"We are what we think,
All that we are arises with our thoughts.
With our thoughts we make the world.
Speak or act with a pure mind and happiness will follow you,
as your shadow, unshakeable."
The Dhammapada {Buddha}

How exactly have I purified my thoughts to have more happiness follow me? How do you clean your house? Like you, I toss out old things (thoughts) that don't work for me anymore or I repurpose things (thoughts) for better results. Why?

❖ What if the average adult has about 50,000 thoughts a day? I was told in a 'Higher Order Thinking' class that approximately 90% of our thoughts are repeated thoughts from the past.

❖ Inaccurate thoughts can create chaotic thinking. You can permanently record within you another person's opinion as a fact. You can record a thought as a fact when it's actually false, and you can record a thought from your childhood that no longer serves you.

❖ Again, If you think "I CAN'T", you have NO chance of success because "I can't" reflects perceived ability; if you think "I WON'T", you have a 10% chance of success because "I won't" reflects conscious choice.

When you only have about 30 seconds to change a thought, think more carefully before it becomes "set", or recorded within your mind. This is how I have learned to manage my current thoughts. What I did was focus on my current thoughts by doing the following.

I asked myself good questions: *What am I thinking?* Is this a thought that helps me be a better thinker? *Is this thought a fact or an opinion?* I can reject opinions from other people that might be meant to make me feel inferior. *Is this an outdated thought?* Sometimes thoughts can become obsolete and no longer serve you.

I decided to write my thoughts in the positive. A goal like "get rid of my debt" uses a negative word—debt. I rewrote it to "I pay my bills on time and have more than enough money," The "debt" did disappear.

I practiced rewording my thoughts out loud. Instead of using "Don't panic!" I reword it to reaffirm what I want—"Calm down."

I started stating my goals in the present tense. "I AM healthy." This way, my thought guides my actions to be more in alignment with a healthy goal.

I decided to be kind to myself with my own thoughts. "I am fat" is not kind! Kind is "I can change my weight by regularly exercising and eating well." When I leave the emotional fat out, I can focus on what I can do.

I decided to let go of worry. I have three siblings that had Alzheimer's. I could get my brain in a tizzy over worrying about getting it myself. I have found their children are also nervous about inheriting it, so I developed a theory about it that I shared with them. I focus on the youngest three siblings, who exhibit no signs of it. (The thought being that the oldest three lived on a farm around dangerous, possibly brain-affecting chemicals that the younger ones did not.) This one thought, even though it's a theory, allays my fear and helps me choose to think well by keeping my brain engaged in healthy activities instead of worrying.

I catch my negative thoughts and tell myself to "CANCEL, CANCEL, CANCEL," then replace it with a positive thought.

Patanjali so eloquently wrote, "When you think inspired thoughts you discover yourself to be a far greater person than you ever <u>dreamed</u> your Self to be." So, DREAM!

How do I get into a dreaming mood? I experience my greater self when I still my mind by focusing on something so Divine—a newborn baby, a beautifully exquisite flower, or a dearly precious loved one—that my heart and mind seem to meld as one. My thoughts seem above this world; and I am, at that moment, in a state of oneness. When I touch others from this space, it is my unconditional love that brings out the best in me and in them.

I finally realize two things:

> **By my willingness to change old thoughts, I opened new doors to life; and I (and you) are worth it! (We** get to graduate to a higher level of thinking**)**

From my experience, there are three things that cost nothing but several minutes a day that made a huge difference in my thought-changing process.

1. The quickest way to raise your thoughts is to replace some of the repeated thoughts from your past.

Steps you would take would be: first, examine why you have a particular reoccurring thought. Second, choose to Cancel, Cancel, Cancel out the thoughts that are inaccurate, are someone else's opinion, or are not relevant anymore.

For example: *My mom said I was an accident waiting to happen! That's because I had a lot of accidents as a child—broken bones, cuts, etc. I got tired of getting hurt and discovered the reason—it was how I got her attention. My mom was a busy woman! I instead decided to think, "To get mom's attention, be attentive to her." You could say I accidentally learned the beauty of treating others the way I wanted to be treated.*

2. Wage a thought campaign on your own or with a friend.

For example: I discovered I was being hard on myself with my own thoughts of me. I was working on the computer and caught myself thinking, *"I'm an electronic idiot!"* Thinking back, it was what I had been telling myself for a long time. I had to catch the thought and change it to *"I've improved my skills with the computer!"* I have. Yee haw!

3. Each day, take at least 20 minutes to still your mind completely!

Stop thinking by focusing on your breathing—slowly breathe in and breathe out for at least 10 breaths and then just be. Choose a mantra like, "Be still and be", or "I am happy right now". Say it over and over again until your mind does what you say. It will calm runaway thoughts and give you a chance to choose new thoughts. Use creative visualizations. When words don't work, picture yourself by a lake and feel the heat of the sun on your face; you could imagine yourself peacefully drifting down a river on a raft, or imagine yourself lying in the grass watching the night sky. Those images can still your mind and calm your thoughts and emotions.

> **"Watch your thoughts for they become your words,**
> **Watch your words for they become your actions,**
> **Watch your actions for they become your character,**
> **Your character becomes your destiny." Frank Outlaw**

Since you know more about energy and thoughts, what could possibly get in your way? **EMOTIONS!** The dictionary says emotions are heightened feelings and agitation caused by strong feelings! Emotions can cause physiological changes in pulse rate and body temperature.

Emotional responses are caused by external motivation or are the result of a past memory or an association to something from your past or through introspection. Just in case you wanted to know, the most common emotional reactions are anger, fear, and love. Becoming emotionally mature can be as simple as raising your own emotional awareness.

When I read the book and took a class on Daniel Goleman's book, Emotional Intelligence, I really agreed with his premise that emotions can make a big difference in people's lives. You and I can raise our Emotional Intelligence, which is a different way of being smart.

His theory on Emotional Intelligence smacked me in the face when I read one of the first questions he asked: "Why do some high IQ people fail and some low IQ people succeed?" I was once married to a very high IQ man and he did fail emotionally; in fact, he died when he was 36 years old. My first husband was smart, but not necessarily smart with impulse control, social deftness, empathy, or self-awareness. He was a perfectionist, to the point that he was an idealist who could not come to grips with normal human nature. He died of alcoholism.

My dad used to say that my first husband was "Too book smart and too life dumb." Dad and Daniel Goleman were and are pretty smart men, emotionally! I had a little knowledge about emotions. My mom taught me to count to 10 when I was angry. Unknowingly, she had showed me how to get from the primitive emotion center, the amygdala, to the rational emotion center. The primitive center is found in the limbic system and is the storehouse of emotional memory where passion and affection come from. It can override any rational thought and is often called the "fight or flight emotional brain".

The rational emotion center is in the neocortex. This thinking emotion brain is what separates man from other animals. Your thinking emotional center can sense slight differences, complex emotions, and you can have feelings about your feelings. Unfortunately, the primitive center can hijack the rational when you experience extreme emotions!

How do we regularly stay rational?

- *Age and experience help.* You and I can learn from our own past and observe people with Emotional Intelligence. Maturity expands perspective.

- *Learn to choose from the wide range of available emotions.* Am I happy, thrilled, or elated? Even though they seem similar, the slight differences create a healthier range of emotions.

- *Learn to clearly state how you feel.* I'm not mad, I'm disappointed. To differentiate, we must first rationally know how each emotion feels.

- *Become aware of your muscles.* Is your fist clenched right now? Does your jaw hurt? Muscles tightening are the first sign of emotional change.

- *Realize drama is a genre like comedy or fiction.* You don't have to be dramatic and can slow down to act instead of react.

- *Know that emotional hijackings can be less disruptive when you are balanced.* I'm certainly less affected when I eat well and get adequate sleep and exercise.

- *Take deep breaths and take stress- and thought-releasing breaks to still emotions.*

I have a responsibility to guide my emotions when working with children. Behavior modification techniques—like rewards and time outs—do work with children. To get attention and much-needed love, children will first choose primitive emotions. Time outs help them and can help us center our emotions back to the rational. Rewards are a recognition and celebration of healthier choices.

As I said earlier, the most common emotions that negatively affect our thoughts and choices are fear, worry, and anger. What does fear do to you? Don't get me wrong—fear can be useful in dangerous situations. However, how often are you in danger? Most often fear comes from past negative experiences. I nearly drowned when I was younger. When I learned how to swim, I replaced that sinking fear by having faith in my abilities to stay afloat.

Do you realize worry and anger are a choice? When you worry, your thoughts are in the future. What if...? Will she be okay? When you are angry, your thoughts are in the past. Why me? I can't believe he did that to me again? #%&⋆! (Did I just swear?)

Is staying in the present moment my best choice then? For me it is, unless I start "should"ing on myself. I inherited that emotional disease from my parents. I *should* finish this now; I *should* stop and say hello even though I'm late. These emotional reactions came from past experiences and cultural expectations. Emotions punctuate our thoughts. Doubt? Excitement! Frustration (ARG) It is the emotion behind thought that causes words and deeds to be misinterpreted.

What if you think it is okay to say or do one thing, and another person thinks that same thing is not okay? This is what causes conflict that can develop into harassment or punishable crimes. I go with what I once read as a universal law: "Do what you will, but harm no one!" Most agree harm is physically, mentally, or emotionally abusing someone else. If you are doing something to me against my free will and I have asked you to stop, then I am being harmed, even if you don't agree.

How often have you heard, "Sticks and stones can break my bones but words can never hurt me?" Ill-chosen thoughts spoken with great emotion **can hurt**. If you choose to let them, they can be harmful. However, **you can refuse to accept ill-spoken words**. Ask the person to stop or walk away.

> "An arrow may fly through the air and leave no trace,
> But an ill thought leaves a trail like a serpent."
> Charles Mackay

What have I done to alter my emotions to improve the impressions I leave on others?

Have you ever been yelled at? Do you have to overlook dripping sarcasm or tip-toe around bad moods? That is not fun! Poor emotional expressions also leave a trail like a serpent on those around you! To improve my emotional expression, I do the following.

- **Realize that the driving force of any emotion is intention.**
  Intention is like a motive or plan—a piece of your own attitude. Are you yelling to gain control of a dangerous situation? That

is the only time I should be yelling, I've decided. The message I am sending with this thought is "I care." Am I yelling to win an argument? The message I am sending is "I'm right and I don't care about you."

- **Separate actions from the Self.** I can be mad at someone's actions but still love and believe in him or her. My anger at the action does not affect a person's self esteem if I state my feelings calmly.

- **State things clearly.** Instead of saying, "Don't leave your clothes on the floor!" I say, "When you leave your clothes on the hallway floor, it's dangerous for others." "When you," focuses on a cause/effect.

- **Remain conscious of your emotions by watching reactions.** You will get what you give!

- **If you change the way you look at things, the things you look at change.** I used to feel hurt by one friend's words and actions. I decided to change how I looked at it. Instead of instantly feeling like I did something wrong and I had to fix it, I let it go. The hurtful words and actions went away because I no longer reacted to them. This "friend" then chose to go invalidate someone else.

- **Notice qualities you admire in others.** You can review words and actions of people who treat you well. Ask yourself, "What emotional expression works well for them?" You can choose to develop your own positive qualities for greater results.

- **Strive to pass on your good moods.** Sometimes, when we feel emotionally harassed, we emotionally harass others. The negative boomerang affect can and will continue until you choose to stop it.

Hopefully, you now know more today than you did yesterday. As a parent, teacher, and leader, that is all we can do—educate our Selves for our better tomorrows and for our children's better tomorrows.

> **"I will study and get ready, and**
> **perhaps my chance will come."**
> Abraham Lincoln

CHAPTER 9

The Ninth Key for Better Tomorrows: Commit to Loving the Child within You So You Can Inspire the Child in front of You

Are you perfect yet? Me neither! Should we give up? After all, even though I know more today than I did yesterday, it seems to me that there is just so much more out there to know. However, I'm not striving to be perfect. Instead, I'm striving to make the world a better place by focusing on the world's greatest resource—children. Would you believe that even as a grandparent, I'm still learning to love the child within me? My grandchildren have actually expanded my vision of who I am. By choosing to inspire them, I've encouraged my Self to keep growing.

I used to get smug about knowing all I know now and it was usually a child that put me in my place. For example: *At the beginning of the year, I took my students outside for a science lesson. They had a six-foot piece of string they were to put in a circle—just off the edge of the playground in a more wooded area. They had a paper and pencil and were to write down everything they saw in that circle (mini ecosystem).*

I had a student teacher that year. We were standing around and observing how they were choosing to proceed with their research and recording (watching how they learned) when one boy came up with a hand full of weeds and asked, "Is this poison ivy?"

My answer was a quick, "You'd better hope not!"

His eyes got wide and he dropped the weeds. I quickly looked at them and told him they were not. If they had been, we would have certainly been sorry he had held them in his hands. My student teacher and I quietly chuckled after the child had rather sheepishly walked away.

I started to think. What if there was poison ivy around? I had assumed an area so close to the school playground would have been sprayed during the summer and free of harmful weeds. I asked my student teacher to look around and make sure there was no poison ivy in the area.

Guess what? There was. Now, who was sheepish!

I asked everyone to pick up their circles and we went inside and all washed our hands. I sent my student teacher up to the office to let them know there was poison ivy near the playground. The kids often chased balls that strayed into that area!

Needless to say, I was very grateful to the child who knew about poison ivy and asked about it. I wish I personally would have thanked him that day for saving me from a possible nightmare—it could have cost both the school district and me a lot of embarrassment and headaches!

Why didn't I thank him that day? Actually, his uninhibited reaction of picking and holding on to the possible poison ivy was something I would have done as a child. My thoughts immediately went to the past and myself as a child. I wasn't thinking about how my student was feeling, I went to runaway thought syndrome. I was envisioning the newspaper headline: "Teacher Fired for Exposing 100 Children to Poison Ivy". Drama thoughts!

I hate to admit it, but that's where my thoughts went at the time. I was revisiting my past when I, as a child, was told (sometimes through imaginary newspaper headlines) how my actions could affect me or the family negatively. My parents were trying to impress on me, through fear, a better way to be. I found out many years later that their fear was I would have to endure some of the things they had to endure as children that were very painful to them. Once I finally figured out my parents' motive, it helped me understand them better and I actually grew to really appreciate and love the little boy and girl they once were even more. However, do you and I really need to parent or teach or lead from our past pain? Fortunately, we live in a world where we know more now than we did then.

What does knowing more look like? When my 13-year-old grandson misbehaves, I tell him my dad would spank him for that behavior or that I would have grounded his step-mother for that same behavior. As a grandma, I get to teach. I start by telling him I love him, and then I tell him his current behavior is beneath him. I go back to the lovable, capable, responsible self esteem builders. I ask him how he fell short and give him some concrete suggestions for improvement.

For instance, one day he got angry at me because I reminded him to do a job his dad had left on a list for him to do.

He started yelling at me, slamming doors, and throwing his dad's tools around. Hmmm, was he responsible? His behavior didn't qualify! Then he started to yell at his sisters. Was he lovable? Not hardly! I had to take one of the girls to swim team practice, so I took all of the girls. When we got back, he was calm enough to talk with.

*I'll be darned if I didn't hear myself bring up the word **reputation**, after we had covered the lovable and responsible parts of his behavior. As a grandma, I want my grandchildren to have choices. If he continues with this behavior, he could lose the right to choose at some point.*

It reminded me of the last time my dad spanked me (at age 12); I had told my mom I wouldn't vacuum the house when she asked me to. I never refused to do a chore again after my spanking. My mom and dad knew refusing to help out was not good for my character. Character is not only your personality and nature; it is your moral fiber, charm, integrity, temperament, disposition, spirit, and reputation. My parents were smart enough to know they would not be doing me a favor by letting my refusal to help slide by.

I can't remember specifically choosing to build up my character. I mean, why would it be important to a 12 year old? CHOICE. When I told my mom no, I was making a choice that made me feel like the little girl in me was not as lovable. I was certainly not charming and my temperament was not attractive at that point in time.

To tell you the truth, I've learned over the years that character is very important. Character is not about me doing everything I or someone else tells me to do, it is about learning to choose when to step up to the plate and when to pass on an opportunity. Some opportunities can help us grow, some can limit our choices, and others can create holes in our characters—much like a black hole in space that sucks the matter out of everything (and you end up feeling empty).

As an adult, if I have difficulty knowing when to pass on a shaky opportunity to keep my character strong, how can I teach a child to pass on shaky opportunities? Role models! It is important for a child to develop his or her own character. Sometimes it's not so much about directly teaching, leading, or parenting; it is about modeling good character. What a commitment!

You and I sign contracts (which are commitments) for a job, to buy a house or a car, or to hire some services. Does a leader, like the President of the United States, sign a contract? No; however, the president does swear on a Bible to commit to the responsibilities of the office. I signed a contract to be a public school teacher. I was required to have a teaching certificate and to teach the required curriculum. If I didn't fulfill my responsibilities as a teacher, I could be fired.

You probably didn't sign a contract or even become certified to become a parent! What's true for me? My own character usually guided how I worked with my child, step children and grandchildren. Most parents choose to discipline their child/children using a combination of the same strategies they themselves were raised with. As a result, our own past experiences really affect how we parent.

Which would you rather model for the child in front of you—positive, negative, or indifferent discipline techniques? Like me, you probably experienced all of these styles as a child, which is why we can unintentionally replicate some of those negative/indifferent experiences to our own children. Students of all ages (children and adults in new situations) are good at imitating behavior. I reviewed the discipline styles I endured as a child before choosing my behavior techniques as a parent/teacher. For example, I'll never shut a child in a dark closet (like I was in speech class), but I have sent a grandchild to her own room for a time out. Why? I want the children I touch to reach their tremendous potential and I don't want to be the cause of a trauma that could affect their growth (putting a hole in the work of art in front of me).

My teammates and I would get excited thinking about what our students would choose to do. What if Jeff became President of the

United States? What if Emily became our doctor and Sara ended up teaching our grandchildren? While none of my former students have become a president (yet), several are doctors and teachers.

I recently took my granddaughter back to Lincoln, Nebraska. It is my hometown and she needed a state for a project in social studies. She took pictures of the capital building and was given information for a report. I bring this up now because from my own high school, one student became Nebraska's governor and ran for President of the United States; his sister, a friend of mine in high school, was a state Senator. I used to go to slumber parties at their house!

My granddaughter looked at me in awe! "Grandma, you went to school with a governor and a senator?" I told her anything is possible—she or one of her friends could "become influential", so to speak. For the first time, she realized SHE could be a person that could make a difference for a lot of people—in a good way. She truly has the heart for it.

Considering that she (like you) has some personality traits that are genetically inherited, some that are passed from generation to generation, and some that are developed as a result of her environment—the environment becomes the wild card for all of us! It can make or break a child's life, like a sudden change because of circumstances (war, a lost job, a loved one's death).

Can I let go of some of my past environmental child discipline models and grow to a kinder, more thoughtful way to be with children? I can. I was lucky enough to have multiple opportunities to learn and grow. As a teacher, I could either keep repeating what already was or change to something new.

My parents were great parents, but had a "spare the rod, spoil the child" philosophy. What does that mean? My dad was originally a teacher, a principal, and superintendent of a few school districts. Back then, one of the tools for disciplining children in his office was a paddle. It was not unusual to paddle a child who was misbehaving. Actually, a generation later, my husband was also a principal—he, too, had a paddle in his office and used it on occasion.

Today, two of my former teammates are the principals of my grandchildren's schools. There is no paddle in sight in their offices. In fact, they themselves are out in the hallways, in classrooms, and in the lunchroom interacting with students rather than sitting in their offices. They know every student and take care of potential problems on the spot in a caring way. When they have to, they use behavior modification techniques like time outs and rewards. The bottom line is they have grown into a better way of being with children in education. They model good character.

What is the result of a constant presence with good character—like my two former colleagues? My grandchildren love to go to school. My granddaughter told me she couldn't wait for Mondays, and I asked her why. She said, "I get to go to school and learn!" (Yes, she really said that about school.) I think she feels safe and special at school!

My 13-year-old grandson looks forward to seeing his principal and teachers. He knows they want him to succeed and will pay attention to him. My friend substitute teaches in his school. She just told me my grandson walked into her classroom while she and another teacher were talking between classes; he joined in the conversation in an appropriate manner and was adorable. He looks forward to seeing his classmates, teachers and principals; he's learning AND he's happy.

Do you tend to discipline the child in front of you like your parents did you or are you changing to meet your child of today's needs? Today's children are no different than you and I were as children. I behaved better when I felt loved, when I felt my parents and teachers believed I was capable, and when I was taught how to be responsible. Today's children are also different in a way. Because of technology, there is so much more data available to them at an earlier age. My granddaughter taught me how to use my "smart" phone (no wonder some parents discipline by taking away their children's phones!) How do I discipline her when she thinks she is smarter than me at times? I model good character!

My step-daughter and I were talking recently— I asked her for some computer help. Seven years ago, she was the head of the technology department for a corporation. However, she said she could no longer help me because computers had changed so much since she worked with them. However, my granddaughter, who is nine, did help me! How? While she may not know exactly how, **she was not afraid to try.**

If you and I always do what we always have done, we will always get what we always got. Don't be afraid to try to do something different!

I was forced into trying something different as a parent. Put a teenage girl with a single mother working two jobs and what do you get? I got a teenage girl who wanted to "parent" herself and me. Truthfully, she was a better at it in the beginning. I was barely treading water. However, as time passed, I realized I was not doing her any favors. Maybe it was because she was sleeping in, forging my signature, and arriving at school late, missing some of her classes. That was not my definition of responsible. What did I do? I had to look at the choices I was making that affected her in a negative way. My own self esteem was so low; I was not a good role model.

Since others perceive my character from my personality, what did I try? I boosted my self esteem enough to enrich my character so I could be a better role model.

I reviewed my inner most feelings and truths. I made a commitment to be who I am and to stand up for what I believe in. I decided to speak and act in a way that reflected my values.

I widened my view of who I am. I honored my talents and developed complimentary traits to expand my horizons. I learned new skills to strengthen weaknesses and practiced using them well.

I validated my Self. I gave up comparing myself to others! I decided to practice humility, gentleness, and unconditional love, starting with myself. I chose to think every past experience, relationship, and hardship has made me who I am today.

I chose to be a parent, leader, and teacher (a storyteller); not a preacher.

I realized each day is a new day and I had the power to make it special. The present moment is the greatest gift I have and every success, no matter how great or small, is a wonder.

I raised my Emotional Intelligence and became more "energy wise" by purposefully altering my attitude.

My favorite attitude adjustments from that time in my life are:

Choose an attitude of gratitude. If I am grateful for what I have, I will find more things to be grateful for.

Accept challenges gracefully. I look at a challenge as a test of my abilities. Challenges happen for everyone, and it stimulates growth.

Choose to surrender at one moment to create success in another moment. I do that by giving up the need to be right. Being right isn't always important, especially when I'd rather be happy!

Give up savior mentality. Sometimes I try and "save the day." When I consistently try to save a person or situation, I can interfere with the lessons they may need to learn in life.

Develop a greater sense of humor. I can learn to smile inwardly or laugh outwardly to defuse stress or gain perspective.

Gracefully accept disappointment. If I lose a promotion or something I really want, I think something better will come along for me.

Remember, "While it is nice to be important, it is more important to be nice."

I inherited my parents' inner compass to living life. *When my father passed away, one of his colleagues sobbed inconsolably. He apologized to my mom for how he had treated my dad. (He had deliberately undermined my dad on occasion because he wanted my dad's job.) Even I had noticed it and had asked my dad why he didn't call this man out on his behavior. My dad said, "Just you wait and see."* It was about 15 years later the health teacher from my school went to a regional health educator's conference. This same man was retiring . . . the qualities they honored him for, were the qualities my dad modeled for him! I could feel my dad's smile.

So, when I am unsure of myself, I ask myself the question, "What would Jesus do?", or "what would my dad do?" When I think of the actions of a higher power or a person I hold in high esteem, I teach my Self to choose higher or better thoughts and actions. **I also choose to believe in serendipity or coincidence or good fate.** The belief in 'good things can happen to good people' brings out better thoughts and actions in me and inspires greater-than-me thinking. I can aspire to inspire others, like my parents did.

By believing in a higher power, good fate and the natural rhythm of life, I can trust divine rightfulness will eventually happen. I do not have to feel hurt or wronged. Justice will prevail at some point in time. I have learned to let things go and go with the ebb/flow theory.

When you look in a mirror, your reflection varies from day to day. I have learned to look at others' words and actions as a reflection that also fluctuates. Just as I have wished to take words back, so might someone else. I can choose to not take things so personally when I realize that each personal exchange is teaching me how to be or how not to be.

The relationship I have with others will only be as good as the relationship I have with MY SELF!

What happened when I decided to strengthen my character so I could be better today than yesterday? I discovered that I lost the magic of my thoughts and best intentions when I faced too many criticisms or complaints! I got overly emotional when I was disappointed in my fellow humans. I lost energy when circumstances out of my control overwhelmed me. Even the heartiest of souls can struggle with life lessons—the death of a loved one, the illness of a child, or the sadness of a senseless situation. I have found if I **concentrate on a simple positive action**, my energy and attitude improve, causing possibly better things to happen.

When I am worried about someone or something, my simple positive action is to light a candle or put a picture of them under a light or say a prayer, and ask for the person to be safe and protected. When I am worried about a situation, I write it down and put the paper under or inside of my favorite sacred object and ask for help. When I am worried about a relationship, I put a picture of both of us under a light and ask for the highest good to happen for both of us.

When I feel disharmonious energy and I find myself upset with a person or feeling negative energy in a situation, I say aloud or silently to myself, "Bless Love, Bless Love, Bless Love!" **Then I let it go.** When I feel negative energy directed toward me, I put my hands over my belly just below my waist or if I am seated, I cross my feet and hands and ask to be protected. If the negative energy continues, I visualize myself sitting in a golden pyramid and ask for ONLY positive thoughts to come through to me. When my house feels thick with energetic clutter, I spray sea salts to remove low energy and rose water to replace it with higher energy, or I ring chimes, light incense, or put a high energy crystal out. When I feel unbalanced energy coming at me, I click my fingers to disperse it. These strategies come from my energy education—educational Kinesiology; the dowsers; Anneliese Hagemann, who taught a class I took on the inner art of dowsing (in the search for Health--Happiness--Harmony in Body--Mind--Spirit); and from Reiki and Qi Gong.

Do these simple positive actions work? I find that they take away my frustration and stress, and I become more peaceful. I have a better chance of staying in the moment when I use these techniques. I also have a better chance of making a difference for my child, grandchildren, and the children in front of me.

I once had a student who was adopted from a warring Asian country when he was six months old; the adoption agency had warned the parents this baby was very angry and difficult.

I had this child for both fifth and sixth grade—he was a challenge! We made good progress in the two years I had him; however, I got a call from the seventh grade guidance counselor when he moved to the Junior High. She was furious with him and was asking me for help in working with this child. She was yelling at him and he started clicking his fingers in her face. She was livid.

I had not taught this child to do that, he instinctively knew. I had taken the class that taught me this strategy just the week before she called me. I told her what I learned. She calmed down and realized she would not be able to yell at this child. She further explained she had been pointing her finger at him in a threatening way! She decided to try a different strategy.

This finger-clicking strategy doesn't just work well with people; it can work with places.

When I retired from teaching, I took a fun job at a retail store. My boss was from Minnesota and was part Native American. She had spent summers with her grandmother on the reservation. She was aware of energy. Some days, she would walk in the store and immediately be uneasy; she didn't like the energy, even though the store was clean and straightened.

I taught her to disperse negative energy by clicking her fingers. She was so entertaining as she circled the store dramatically clicking her fingers up and down and all around. The store felt better when she did and more customers seemed to walk through our doors.

What are some simple positive actions I take to build up my energy?

I use visualization techniques and I listen to enlightening music. Kinesthetically, I like being in nature, exercising, lighting candles, and using calming scents like lavender. I also use relaxation techniques like meditating, doing Reiki, or taking a hot bath.

When I feel I will not be listened to or heard in a situation (when I am so angry I know I will cut someone to the quick), I write a detailed note describing my exact feelings and then burn it or crumble it up and drown it. When I want to get something off my chest and I feel I will not be heard, I visualize putting the person or group in a large bubble. I step into the bubble and tell them everything I want to say, and then I step out of the bubble and send them (like a balloon, out of my body, mind, and spirit).

How else do I build positive energy?

Two of my friends and I were invited for supper with one of our mentors, Jerry Hummel.

Jerry wanted us to see his new house. Jerry had a unique perspective on life, so we didn't know quite what to expect. As we followed him from room to room, he said, "In this next room, you get to see the angels." I got goose bumps because Jerry was the kind of man who seemed capable of showing us a real angel. We walked into the next room—the bathroom! He said, "Look in the mirror, and you will see real angels." We looked and saw ourselves. He said, "See, you are angels on Earth that can make this world a better place." He then taught us to tap our breast bone several times and with each tap say, "I love me, I love me, I love me." His theory was that we are all capable of acting like angels and we could start by loving and honoring ourselves.

Since you and I are works of art in progress, how do we get to angel-like thinking? I know my self esteem can dip pretty low now and then. How about you? I was taught in another class to write a letter and read it often. It was a letter to myself detailing how I am capable, lovable, and responsible so that I could keep my own self esteem higher. I was also taught that if I feel overwhelmed by events in my life, to do one nice thing for myself each day until I no longer feel overwhelmed.

We have such a wide variety of emotions; however, I can get stuck on nervous when I start thinking about an upcoming event or big change. Forget angel-like thinking. I learned a technique that not only helped me, it also helped one of my students. In fact, she wrote an essay about it in high school and her father (my principal) shared it with me.

She had just finished two years in our team and we had to clean up after the graduation. Our student, her sister, and her dad were walking out with me. Her sister was holding the helium-filled balloons and one of them escaped from her grasp. It was floating up toward the Junior High my student would be attending the next year.

My student was furious with her sister and started yelling at her. Her dad looked a bit stunned, so I jumped in and said, "Oh no, you need to thank your sister."

*She looked surprised but asked why. I quickly replied, "The balloon is floating toward the building you'll be in next year. That building is attached to the high school. It is a good sign—**your energy is preceding you at your new schools**. Visualize the best happening. All your hopes and dreams can come true if you work hard. That balloon is a sign that these schools are a great place for you to be able to learn the next six years of your life."*

My words had such an impact on her, she was (in an instant) totally able to change her thoughts about her future; she let go of the fear she had been feeling about changing schools. She did thank her sister and her dad thanked me, both then and several years later by showing me her essay on "a moment in her life" that changed her perspective.

I have added several other **"one positive action techniques"** over the years that have helped me. I was able to study and take classes on reflexology after I retired. There are three body parts—your hands, feet, and ears—that have acupressure points corresponding to every organ in your body. My grandchildren's favorites are their ears. They can be totally stressed out, and I will start rubbing their ears. They go to mush and relax pretty fast when I do that.

I learned to spread my fingers apart three times when I want to separate my energy from someone else's. I tend to do that a lot during the day. I was also taught by Dr. Effie Chow that when my energy felt low to stop and imagine a huge zipper in front of me and mentally zip it up from my toes to the top of my head. When I feel anxious and uptight, my chiropractor has me ask myself, "What thought is making this muscle tighten?" I then put a finger on the tightened muscle, hold my breath, and push the muscle for 5 to 10 seconds. When I let my breath out, I let go of the muscle and the thought. I visualize the muscle and my breath releasing the stress attached to the thought.

While all of these strategies help me stay balanced and get perspective, I have been blessed over the years to have many great teachers that have widened my vision for better tomorrows. My youngest older brother was one of my best teachers and one of my favorite people on this Earth. I was heartbroken when he was diagnosed with lymphoma. At one point in time on his journey, I flew back to go with him for a week to the "drip" room (chemotherapy). I initially thought it was a very depressing place to be. However, he looked at it as a chance to have a longer life and he was grateful for the chance! I decided to adopt his thought.

My sister-in-law would pack a big bag of cherries for both of us and off we'd go to the "drip" room for half a day every day. The first day, I asked him to imagine a higher power's hands (God's) holding a pitcher of the purest water ever above his head. I asked him to "see" God's hands pouring this sacred water slowly into his body.

I asked him to "feel" this sacred water washing each cell, each organ, and every part of him, leaving him refreshed and renewed with clean pink cells and healthy tissue. His answer was—I can do that every day! He always had a smile on his face in the "drip" room and lived longer than his doctors ever expected.

During his journey he continued to teach at UNO (University of Nebraska in Omaha). He gave a speech two weeks before he passed away to educators in Chicago about how Nebraska had made the "No Child Left Behind" law better for the children in his state. His hope was that other states would adopt the additions they had made to the law for better tomorrows for their students.

His wish for better tomorrows for children was his passion. He not only continued to work while he was sick, he did everything he could to update their home and spent as much time as he could with his family. He also played guinea pig, trying an experimental drug that could help him or others with the same diagnosis. I watched my brother interact with his children and grandchildren a week before he died. I was in awe of how effortlessly he walked softly in his own shoes during this time. It felt like I was watching a butterfly transform into an angel. That's character! Even in his darkest of days, he had a smile on his face and was an exceptional role model for his children and grandchildren. He touched thousands of people and always believed there was hope for better tomorrows for the future of mankind.

Why did my brother choose that kind of character? Our dad! Our dad was diagnosed with bone cancer and was given a month to live. He lived six months beyond what he was given and modeled these exact things to all six of his children. Modeling character built character in our dad's favorite people in the whole world—his children.

Do we have to think we're dying to have character? Recently, I've heard (several times) the phrase "Live like you are dying!" Isn't that what humans do? To quote a wise nun, "It may be a long time coming, but you can kind of expect it." What if we decide to think we don't necessarily die, we graduate to a new school beyond Earth?

I never made a bucket list, but that doesn't mean I haven't had a great time being retired. I also have to say the most important thing I've been doing since I left teaching is to keep teaching. Now, I get to teach my own grandchildren. I am incredibly lucky to be able to do so. Recently, I was helping my daughter edit a college paper.

My three-year-old granddaughter walked into the room and wanted to sit on my lap. My daughter told her this was her time with her mom, she would have to wait! We chuckled watching her facial expression.

My little granddaughter said, "You mean my grandma is your mom?" She ignored us completely and finally said, "Mom, Grandma is mine now." Priceless! I can hardly wait to see what else she chooses to come up with in her tomorrows. Actually, my daughter understood. When she was growing up, she had a great deal of attention from her grandparents. With her father sick and her mother working full time, her grandparents played a big role in raising her. At the time, my dad was living like he was dying—literally. Because of his bone cancer, a hospital bed was placed in our living room for him to stare out a large picture window. He loved it when my daughter was sick and came to the house for him to babysit. They played checkers together and he would tell her stories about his past. My mom loved it because she got some time to herself. She would take my daughter out to the garden and they would pick fresh food for lunch while Grandpa watched from his window (and napped).

Her other grandparents were just as wonderful. Her dad's dad would walk from their house and pick her up from school if I had a meeting. Her grandma on her dad's side was extremely entertaining. She had probably the greatest influence on my daughter other than me. In fact, my daughter gave her first child this grandmother's first name as a middle name. Her second child was given my mother's first name as a middle name. What an honor for both of them. They deserved it!

I understood, too. My dad's mom lived with us until I was 8; my mom's dad lived with us until I was 12. I'm so grateful I got to know them and learn from them. I can certainly attribute parts of my character to all the grandparents that helped her and helped me. Neither of us would be who we are without the wisdom of all of their influences.

Developing character requires making better choices. The difference between living life in the positive and living it in the negative is only slightly noticeable at first. Living life with a positive attitude, I am a better model for my loved ones. Living life in the negative, I get critical of others. Many of our challenges are because of chronic negative choice; just watch the news. When poor choice is rampant in any environment, it weakens our natural sense of ease, and in due time, it alters our character because of our choice.

Mankind eventually evolves because a person in a family shines like the sun and that light shines on another, and another until a family evolves. Then that family shines on another, and then another, and another... All those families then positively affect their communities, states, and nations. I think my dad knew that when he chose to pass on his shining character. Dad had not received the same kind of love and attention from his own father. He made the choice of passing on the best of his inherited traits and values. Incredible growth can occur when one person takes an opportunity to step up to the plate and shine like my dad did.

Passing on one's shining character reminds me of the Hundredth Monkey Theory. Basically, the story goes that one day, one monkey's food fell in a pond. The monkey ate it and found it was much tastier when the food was washed. He continued to wash his food and other monkeys saw him; they did what he did—washed their food. That continued to happen until the hundredth monkey. When the hundredth monkey washed her food, all monkeys everywhere knew to wash their food. It was like all monkeys adopted a new way of being when that behavior reached a critical mass.

I would love to see some positive "critical mass" behaviors happen for tomorrow's children. From my experience, the greatest gift I can give the children around me is time to listen from my heart so I can expand their perspective. I can show them that they matter and honor their talents and preferences. I can honor their legacies and teach them about the cycles of life. Most importantly, I can keep learning, not just for me, but also for their better tomorrows.

I can't reach every child by myself. Some children will not learn as well from me as they do from someone else. The same is true for everyone who has children. The children in front of me today— my own child, my step-children, my grandchildren, my family's children, my friends' children—I may not be the person they learn best from. I have to rely on you, or him, or her, or them to help them learn and grow. My greatest hope is that you can when I am no longer able.

When my teammate died in the middle of the school year, I was given a choice of telling our students or having the principal doing it. Actually, my teammate had already prepared them.

My teammate had read the book *The Fall of Freddy the Leaf* by Leo Buscaglia to her class. I reread it to her class and mine. It talks about how Freddy was afraid to let go of the tree and disappear into nothingness. None of us disappears into nothingness; we are all recycled into something else.

You see, I believe in an "All Life Is Recycled" theory. Hopefully, it's something better, like you and I graduate to a higher school of learning and can eventually graduate to the point where we could become an Angel, and maybe Freddy the Leaf can become an Angelic oak tree! I think he would like that.

That's my "Several Lifetimes-Cycle" theory. You and I are first recycled back as our own grandchildren's children or my brother's grandchildren's child. Then we come back as many-generations-removed children until we move to an even higher learning school somewhere else—a distant galaxy away. Maybe we could finally evolve from a wise adult stage to the baby Angel stage. One of my favorite children's books is *The Littlest Angel*. He sure got into a lot of trouble, just like I did as a child. I can't even imagine what it would take to reach the wise Angel stage, but I like to think that it's a possibility. There's certainly no one on earth who knows for sure, is there?

There's the best reason of all to be a positive parent, teacher, and leader—because I have a suspicion that you and I will eventually reap what we have sown on our Earth School journey. Let's see, what is my password again? It's not numbers; it's all words because I love words. My password is . . .

**"There is a destiny that makes us brothers
None goes his way alone
All that we sent into the lives of others
Comes back into our own."**

—Markham

Printed in the United States
By Bookmasters